KENT

The Yachtsman's Guide to the Kentish Tidal Waters

Robert Crane BSc, MPhil, Dip Arb

This book is respectfully dedicated to the RNLI upon whom, thank God, I have never yet had to call.

ISBN
0-9551116-2-5 978-0-9551116-2-4

Published by
Robert Crane / New Wave Press – Market Walls, Market Avenue, Chichester PO19 1JU

Designed and printed by
SRP Design and Print - Leigh Road, Chichester PO19 8TU
www.srpress.co.uk

Front Cover
Ramsgate Inner Harbour

Aerial Photographs
Derek Pasquill

Preface

I was drawn to the Kentish waters by my frustration with the crowded – and relatively expensive – waters of Chichester Harbour and The Solent. Initially, it was a matter of exploring the Cinque Ports which resulted in my first book 'Sail the Cinque Ports', but this in turn led me into something of the Kentish maritime history.

My first real exploration was from 1986 in 'Drogo', a dumpy IP24 which took me from Dorset through the south coast and into The Thames; in 1992 I changed her for 'Jemima Puddleduck', a Peter Duck ketch which was ideal for the longer passages, and over some eighteen years she was warmly welcomed in the harbours and marinas through the Kentish and Essex coasts and the Essex rivers, and again into the Thames. With considerable regret I passed her to a new owner in 2010, and my exploration continues in 'Freya', a Colvic 26.

The Kentish waters offer an unusually wide variety of sailing conditions. There is a close sense of historical continuity with the trading and raiding routes, both local and distant, and the shore-based reminders are always to hand; it is worth too, having regard for the rich treasures of the natural habitats, and taking the opportunity of some rewarding but undemanding coastal walks. This book is therefore intended to provide the yachtsman, not simply with formal pilotage, but also with a comfortable sense of familiarity. My twenty or more years exploring the Kentish and Essex waters have given me enormous pleasure, and this book will have fulfilled its purpose if it enhances the pleasure of others.

I wish that I could list individually all those who have supported me in this exercise; there are the harbour masters, marina managers, club secretaries and numerous others who have enthusiastically pooled their local knowledge, to the extent that this is more their book than mine. I also record my sincere thanks to family and friends whose patience has been tested to exhaustion – and particularly to Derek Pasquill, without whom this book would never have been finished.

By the same Author 'Sail the Cinque Ports'
1st edn 2005
2nd edn 2008

Introduction

The purpose of the chartlets, and particularly of the 'Overviews', is to provide the immediate essentials, and they should be read with the formal charts and pilots to hand. To this end, soundings are omitted with reliance simply on the drying, and the two and five metre contours; similarly, latitude and longitude are omitted, as are individual light characteristics [although these are noted in the accompanying text]. The charts accordingly are not for navigational purposes, but to support the textual descriptions.

Yachtsmen are recommended always to prepare their formal passage plan in comfort, rather than when under way! Matters of occasional background interest are reduced to footnotes, so as not to interrupt the sailing directions; if some of the photographs appear a little dull, it is that they merely reflect an English summer.

A comment or two may be helpful to those unaccustomed to exploring creeks. The courses shown as pecked lines on charts should not be taken too seriously; the courses are always changing a little, and the available depth is subject to variations in barometric pressure and wind. They should always be explored on a rising tide, leaving time for retracing the track; an early, and firm, decision needs to be made as to the safe clearance beneath the keel, having regard to the nature of the bottom, the type of vessel, and weather conditions; bilge-keel craft also need to be aware of the position of the depth transducer in relation to the keels. A little patience opens up new horizons.

The customary cautions are made, in that no responsibility is accepted for errors or misdescriptions; readers' corrections are always welcome. I have given considerable thought to the gazetteer content, which was welcomed in my previous book; it is now on a broader base with less danger of becoming outdated during the course of publication. I also add that recommendations – or otherwise – are based solely on personal experience.

Robert Crane
Chichester, August 2014

Dartford
Gravesend
ROCHESTER
Chatham
Sheerness
Sittingbourne
Conyer
Faversham
Whitstable
Herne Bay
Margate
Broadstairs
RAMSGATE
CANTERBURY
MAIDSTONE
Fordwych
Sandwich
KENT
DOVER
Folkestone
Rye
N
EASTBOURNE

Contents

The South Coast
Overview 9
Rye 15
Folkestone 25
Dover 29

The Forelands
Overview 37
Sandwich 43
Ramsgate 49
Broadstairs 55

The North Coast
Overview 59
Margate 65
Herne Bay 69
Whitstable 73

The Swale
Overview 77
Faversham 83
Conyer 89
Milton Creek 93
Queenborough 95

The River Medway
Sheerness to Rochester 101
Gillingham 111
Chatham 115
Stangate and Half Acre Creeks 119
The Hoo Flats 123
Rochester to Allington Lock 129

The Kentish Thames
Oaze to Dartford Creek 139

APPENDICES
I Distances 147
II Tidal Differences, Streams & Curves 148
III Navigational Aids 154
IV Some Useful Contacts 156
V About the Author 158

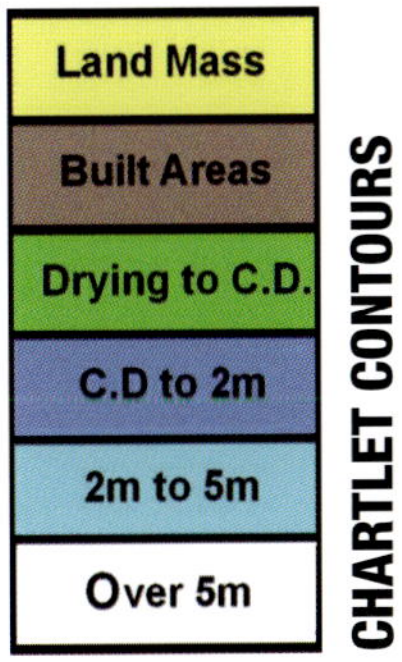

SOUTH OVERVIEW	MARITIME INFORMATION
CHARTS	Admiralty SC5605 / 6A, 7; Imray 2100.5,6,7
TIDAL DIFFERENCES [approx] on DOVER	Rye Harbour 0000; Rye Strand Quay +0010 Folkestone -0010; Sheerness +0130; Tilbury +0240
COASTGUARD	DOVER Ch 69 16, 80 [01304 210008]
HARBOUR MASTERS	RYE [Rye Harbour Radio] Ch14 [01797 225225] FOLKESTONE Ch 15 [01303 254597] DOVER Ch 74 [01304 240400]

SOUTH OVERVIEW	WAYPOINTS
Sovereign Harbour Safe Water Mark	050⁰47'.35N; 000⁰20'78E
Rye Fairway	050⁰54.04N; 000⁰20'.78E
Dungeness South Cardinal	050⁰54'.85N; 000⁰57'.51E
CS3	050⁰21'.02N; 001⁰02'.15E
Folkestone Pierhead	051⁰04'.56N; 001⁰11'.72E
Dover Harbour, Western Entrance	051⁰06'74N; 001⁰19'.73E
Dover Harbour, Eastern Entrance	051⁰07'.25N; 001⁰20'61E

DUNGENESS PANORAMA

The South

OVERVIEW

The southern coastline is fully exposed through southwest to southeast, and there is no all-tide safe haven between Eastbourne's Sovereign Marina and Dover; the Sovereign Marina entrance is not recommended under very severe conditions; at Dover, assistance may be called for if necessary. Rye provides a limited haven for entry at around high water; shelter may also be found in the lee of Dungeness, where there is good holding in sand. Some shelter may be found in the lee of Folkestone pier, although subject to surge and consideration of both depths and quality of holding [an anchor ball or riding light must be shown, and a tripping line for the anchor would be sensible], but the approach here is potentially dangerous.

Yachtsmen should be aware of the Traffic Separation Zone [TSZ], which passes within 3nM off Dungeness. Unplanned incursion may meet with severe penalties, as well as confrontation with southbound traffic.

Weather

The climate is predominantly Atlantic, with prevailing southwesterlies, and with a long fetch.

This makes for easy eastwards passage making, but can be very laborious for a westwards passage with wind over tide; weather conditions are usually predictable, but can change significantly during a passage of around 50nM from, say, Dover to Eastbourne.

Tides

The tidal streams generally parallel the coast and are not strong; the tide makes to the east and, for ease of identification, the charted tidal diamonds A, B, and D are shown within the 'Inshore Passage'. The strongest tide is off Sandgate Road at HW Dover [2.2, 3.9] when the tide is making, but otherwise the streams seldom exceed 1kt; on the eastbound tide, there is slack water south of Dungeness at HW Dover +3, moving to Sandgate Road at HW Dover+4; on the ebb, there is slack water at Sandgate Road at HW Dover -2, moving to the Forelands at HW Dover -1.

The tidal streams make only a moderate incursion into Rye Bay, but are still sufficient to provide uncomfortable conditions in heavy weather; the Dungeness promontory deflects the tidal stream cross-channel towards *CS3* marking the TSZ, and slow moving craft should be aware of this, particularly on the ebb at Dover HW -3.

Eastbourne to Dungeness

Three alternative tracks, eastbound from Sovereign Marina safe water mark *[LFl 10s]* towards Rye Bay, are shown for convenience; they, and their distances, are approximate.

There is the anecdote of a yachtsman caught in fog just off Dover Harbour, and feeling his way by hand along the Southern Breakwater. This is not recommended practice.

SUMMARY NOTES on TRACKS

A, B, C are the direct passages from / to Sovereign Harbour [Eastbourne] safe water mark [050047'.35N; 000020'78E]

A: To Rye Fairway on 0690T [2490T], 18nM. This passes close to the rock outcrops east of Hastings, and within the 2m depth contour.

B: To Dungeness South Cardinal on 0730T [2530T], 25nM. This crosses the Lydd Firing Range, and is subject to the overfalls at Dungeness.

C: To about mid-way between Dungeness and CS3 [TSZ] on 0760T [2560T], 26nM; this is a clear passage.

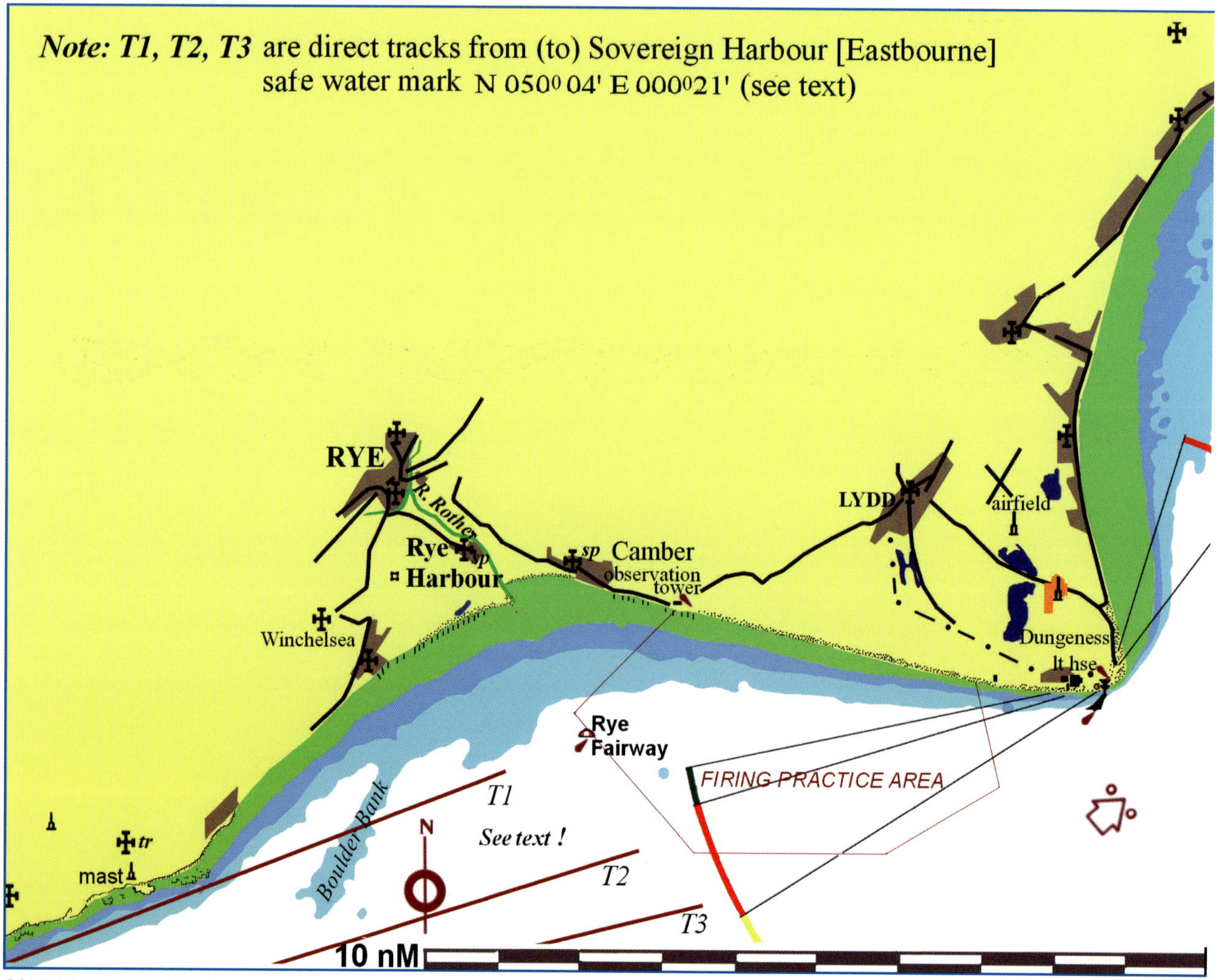

SOUTH OVERVIEW – West

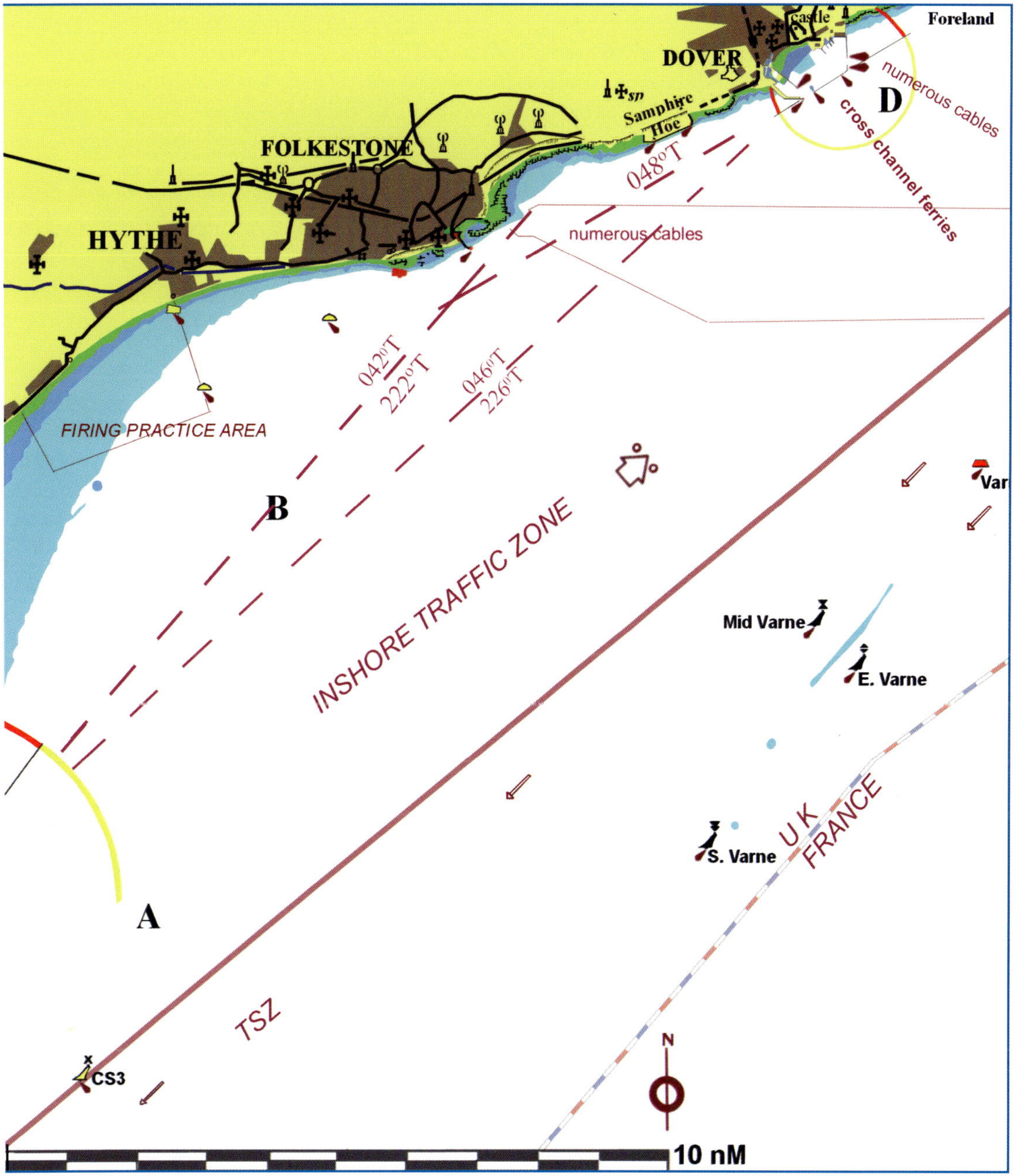

SOUTH OVERVIEW – East

Track '*T1*' is direct to ***Rye Fairway*** *[RW, LFl 10s]* [069°T / 249°T, 18nM]; it should be adopted with caution, as it passes within the 2m depth contour at Fairlight and again within Rye Bay. On passage, Hastings Pier *[FlR 2.5s]* is to be avoided; eastwards, it parallels the steep-to shingle beach, until the two easternmost breakwaters are passed, with the white rectangular building of the Hastings Motor Boat and Yacht Club on the shore between and behind. The coastline continues to close with two small bays of changing depths beneath the chalk cliffs, until the eastern head of Fairlight Bay marks the commencement of Rye Bay; this provides little shelter from the south and west, and can be inhospitable in rough conditions.

Fairlight Knoll, off Fairlight Head, is within a charted depth of 5m, and at the western end of Rye Bay is the tongue of Boulder Bank and Tower Knoll with charted depths of 3m and 2m respectively; within Rye Bay, care should be taken not to confuse the deeper water between Boulder Bank and the shoreline, with that in Rye Bay itself. The sands, throughout the bay, are prone to shifting, and there are numerous fishing nets.

This inshore passage would only be of interest to those making for Rye but, as that entrance is only open for a couple of hours either side of High Water, the depths offshore at Fairlight may not be critical; close inshore however, beam seas will be experienced except under the most favourable conditions, and small craft will find it more comfortable on a parallel course at about a half-mile off, turning in for Rye Fairway only when the last headland is abeam.

The shoreline from Fairlight to the entrance to the River Rother is mostly rocky before giving way to the sea wall of Winchelsea beach. The high point of Fairlight Down is in transit with the church tower beneath on 271°T and Rye church tower [together with a smaller spire behind] can be a good daymark if there is not too much haze.

THE DUNGENESS HORN is a stark cuboid on the beach

ROMNEY -THE ENTRANCE TO THE CHURCH OF ST. NICHOLAS: The tide-mark on the pillars is that left by the flood water and is visible throughout the Church

To the east of the river entrance is the sweep of Camber Sands beach, with the leisure area behind; if inshore beware of swimmers and toy craft; the coastguard should be advised if they are dangerously offshore. There is a seasonal line of yellow buoys off Camber beach, about on the LW line, marking the swimming area, and vessels are requested not to pass inshore of these.

The eastern side of the bay approximately parallels the line of electricity pylons leading from Dungeness power station, well lit at night, with Lydd airfield behind. Anchoring here is in sand and sandy shingle; it is a matter of preference as to depth but, the closer inshore, the more that care needs to be taken of wind shifts.

Track '*T2*' is direct to the Dungeness south cardinal *[Q(6)+LFl]* [073°T / 253°T, 25nM], and on this passage there is the minimum charted depth of 5m off Sovereign Harbour and again off Fairlight Bay. Hastings Pier leading lights will be observed on 356°T; the Fairlight radio mast *[RG]* and church tower are on about E 0°38.5', but are not visible from a small boat on Track 'T1'.

The track crosses the Lydd Firing Range; when in use a red flag is *usually* flown from the look-out post on the shore. The range is for small-calibre weapons, and times of firing are accordingly not transmitted on 'SUB/GUNFACTS'; Rye Harbourmaster has again been included in the listed firing times; information *may* also be obtainable from Dover CG [Ch16]. A fast patrol boat will escort traffic away from the area when in use, notwithstanding it being technically one of free passage. At Dungeness, the power station is an imposing structure just

The town of Romney, one of the Cinque Ports, was situated on the old course of the River Rother; progressive silting occasioned the building of New Romney downstream. In the storm of 1284, the River Rother changed its course overnight, leaving the town high and dry; it is now some two miles inland.

above the steep-to shingle foreshore, with the line of pylons leading north-west; the south cardinal marks the power station outfall. There are overfalls at the point, varying in strength with tide and weather; they are practically unavoidable by closing inshore. To the east are the old lighthouse [black] and the 'new' [black/white] *[Fl 10s and Fl RG + horn]*; the horn is a squat 6m cuboid on the beach. The east facing shore is also of steep-to shingle, and with inshore fishing boats drawn up.

Track '*T3*' is direct to about midway between Dungeness south cardinal [076°T / 256°T, 26nM] and *CS3 [Fl Y 10s + Bell]* marking the TSZ. There is a minimum charted depth of 5m off Fairlight Bay, but otherwise the passage is clear. The comments above regarding Dungeness and the TSZ should be noted.

Dungeness to Dover

The direct passage – The Inshore Traffic Zone - has a minimum charted depth of 13m with a predominantly sandy bottom upon which there are numerous wrecks, and even more numerous power cables running about 090°T just north of Folkestone.

To the east of Dungeness, the ensuing bay [East Road to Sandgate Road] finds the Hythe firing range; comments apply as for the Lydd range [above]; the eastern extremity is marked by two Martello towers on the shoreline, beyond which is a lookout tower [from which a red flag *should* be flown]; there is an inshore yellow buoy *[Q, Y]* and another offshore *[FlY, 5s]*. The shoreline here is gently shelving, with the potential for sheltered anchoring in predominantly firm sand, changing to predominantly mud further offshore. The numerous Martello Towers are generally not good landmarks, because of the difficulty in individual identification.

The shoreline east of Hythe gives way to cliffs with rock outcrops. There is currently no ferry service out of Folkestone, but there is still the occasional visiting commercial vessel. To clear Folkestone Harbour a back bearing of better than 222° T from Dungeness lighthouse must be maintained until the southern breakwater of Dover Harbour *[Oc R 30s / Fl(4) WR 10s]* is in transit, bearing 048°T [238°T]; this course leads into the Dover Harbour small craft holding area [west].

The course of 042°T [222°T] from Dungeness to the intersection with the Dover transit also provides a suitable initial approach for Folkestone Harbour; anchoring near the entrance is not a good option other than in an emergency.

The direct course, for Dover Harbour western entrance from Dungeness lighthouse, is on a bearing of 048°T [228°T]. There are very frequent ferry services out of Dover, for which a good lookout must be kept. Dover Port Control may be contacted when a mile off [Ch 74], advising them of intentions and seeking advice as to imminent ferry movements; at a half-mile off, a request for entry may be made if so required.

A passage past Dover should be made a mile or so off, to maximise visibility of the numerous ferries; these rapidly attain a speed well in excess of 20kts, and their ability to manoeuvre is limited. Dover Harbour is about 3nM from the TSZ, and anchoring in the vicinity is prohibited.

Samphire Hoe, on the shoreline between Folkestone and Dover, is an artificial leisure area constructed from the spoil of the channel tunnel excavations. Vessels should avoid closing in on the sea wall, as there are protective boulders at the base.

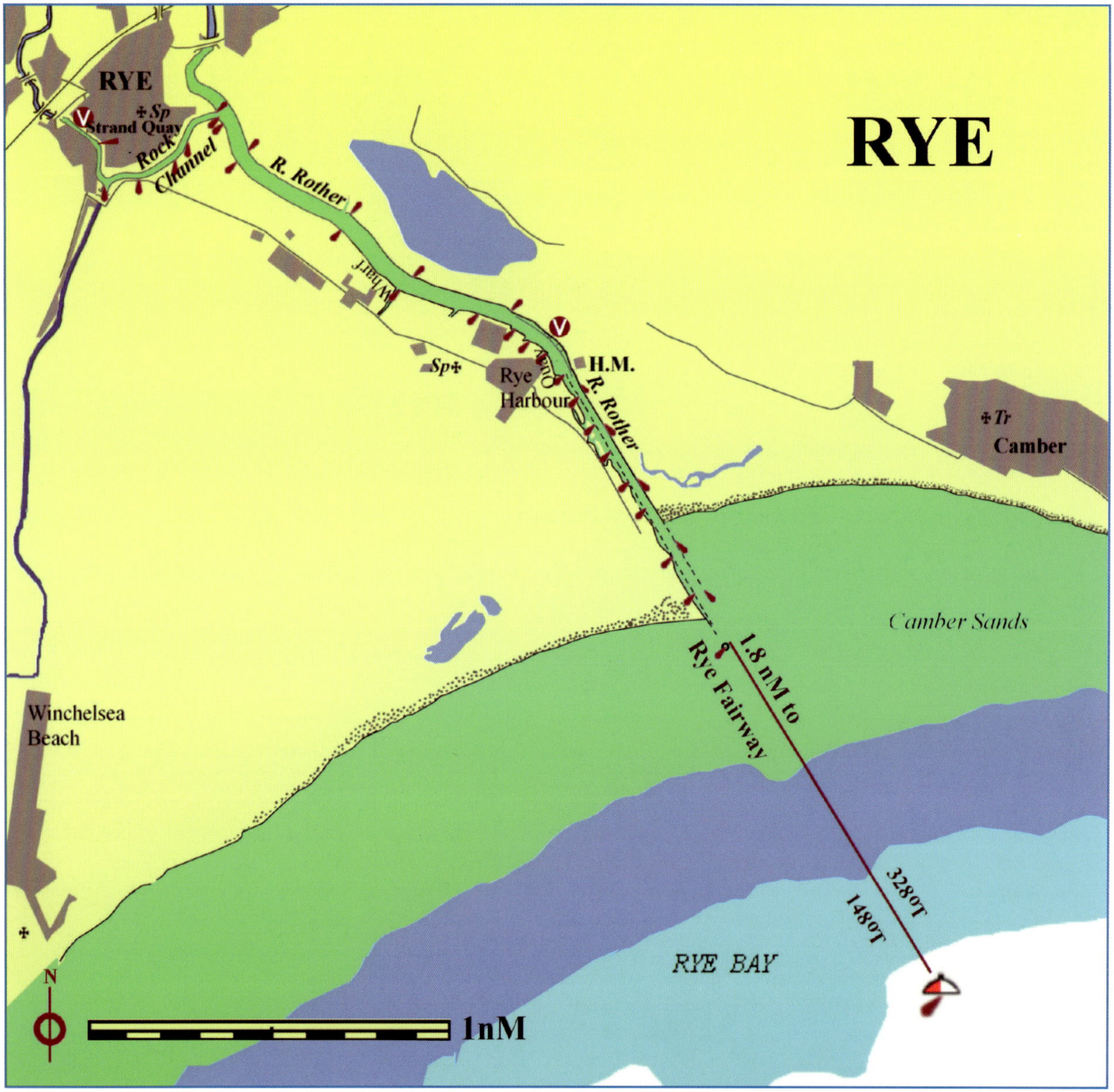

RYE & THE RIVER ROTHER

NOTE: THE TRUE POSITION OF "RYE FAIRWAY" IS OFF CHART

The South

RYE

RYE is included because of its close association, both historical and geographical, with maritime Kent. There was no permanent settlement here until the tenth century, when the township grew on the sandstone bluff above the marshes, defended on three sides by the Rivers Rother, Brede and Tillingham, and the marshland behind. It was the River Rother which enabled its development as an important fishing and trading port, together with shipbuilding and associated industries which continued into the late nineteenth century; it, and the nearby Winchelsea, were the two 'Ancient Towns' as Members of the medieval Cinque Ports whose defensive role was pivotal in enabling England to develop as a nation state.

The town has a rich history with delightful architecture and street scenes. It is easily accessible by road and rail, it is well served commercially and has a generous choice of pubs and restaurants; there are splendid coastal views from the church tower. It is well worth a few days' exploration, notwithstanding the limited berthing.

THE MERMAID HOTEL - The Hotel dates from the fourteenth century and was rebuilt in the sixteenth.

THE VIEW FROM ST. MARY'S CHURCH - The Ypres Castle is in the centre, with Rock Channel behind, and the River Rother beyond.

THE YPRES CASTLE Earlier known as the Baddings Tower

ST MARY'S CHURCH

Navigation and Berthing

Tidal restrictions limit entrance to Rye to between HW-2 and HW+3 but, without local knowledge, it should not be left later than HW+1; it is best to approach from a couple of miles off, and Rye Bay can be unpleasant in strong onshore winds; care should be taken also to avoid numerous anchored nets. Within this tidal range, the approach from the west presents no particular hazards once past the Royal Sovereign Shoals. The approach from the east requires avoidance of the Hythe and Lydd Firing Ranges [see above].

The entrance can be made safely at night and under sail, given reasonable conditions; once inside, it is better to proceed under engine. There is occasional commercial traffic, and the fishing fleet

THE ENTRANCE TO THE RIVER ROTHER AT LWN+1

The village of 'Rye Foreign' was so named because it lay outside the jurisdiction of the Cinque Ports. The town of Winchelsea, perched above the River Brede, was the 12th Century replacement for the 'Old Winchelsea' which had been washed away; it was a major port for the wine trade, but declined with silting of the river.

THE ENTRANCE TO THE RIVER ROTHER AT HWN-1

also; before making the final approach, it is sensible to check the level of activity with the Harbour Master [*Rye Harbour Radio* Ch 14] [not 24hrs, unless commercial traffic is expected].

The inconspicuous entrance is guarded by a crescent of sandbanks just off, and these are always shifting; visibility is often hazy. The approach should be made from ***Rye Fairway*** *[RW, LFl 10s]* [50°53.80N 00°48.13E], and then on a course of 329°T for 1.8nM to leave the western breakwater *No 2* mark *[FlR 5s]* close to port, and this course continues upstream. Until the entrance has been identified, the track from ***Rye Fairway*** should be maintained with a back bearing, but it is better to keep about 10m off *No 2* [see the aerial photograph for the adjoining shallow]. The eastbound flood tide can make over 2kts across the entrance and the westbound a little less; within the channel, both flood and ebb can attain 5kts and this, combined with the cross tides, makes for unpredictable local currents; it is important therefore, to maintain the bearing.

There is a depth gauge on the eastern breakwater structure, comprising three horizontal timbers at 1.5m intervals, commencing at 2.0m above the river bed. Of more practical use is the nearer western [port hand] structure; when its concrete base is covered, there are better than 2.5m of water over the bar but subject to wave height. In severe conditions, the disturbance to the river bed at the entrance makes a depth sounder useless.

With the western breakwater abeam, the eastern breakwater should be identified at some 240m upstream; this may be submerged at HW, but has a steel structure at its head with a green board above, illuminated at night *[Q(9)]*, and opposite this is *No 6 [QR];* the course remains at 329°T to pass midway between the two breakwaters, and is straight for about 0.7nM with the best water in the centre of the channel.

On the port hand, the western breakwater extends upstream into the Training Wall, a continuous structure which is submerged at HW, but which is marked by buoys *[R, unlit]* and withies, and which should be given a decent berth; conditions on the 'wrong' side of the wall are unpredictable at best. Upstream, the wall is continuous with the Town Quay and this is not particularly obvious when submerged at HWS. On the starboard hand, the eastern breakwater continues as a stone revetment, marked by lights *[Fl G]*.

RYE – THE HARBOUR MASTER'S OFFICE

RYE HARBOUR – UPSTREAM

RIVER BREDE MOORINGS

Once between the breakwaters, the harbour is well sheltered except from a strong southerly swell; from here, the visitor should proceed under engine within the speed limit of 6kts, and identify the Harbour Master's Office ahead at about 0.5nM on the starboard bank; this is the first substantial building on that hand, and comprises a modern two-storey structure with radio mast behind. If VHF contact has not already been made, it is now appropriate to do so to confirm the absence of commercial traffic; above the office are IPT Signals *[RRR, GGG]* which, if switched on, must meet with compliance, even if that entails stemming the tide and tucking tightly inshore. The commercial traffic comprises the occasional 25m coaster, and there is also an active fishing fleet; there is room to pass, but with little margin and a lookout astern should be maintained.

The Harbour Office is open during normal working hours, seven days a week, and at other times when there is commercial traffic. Unless prior arrangements have been made, visitors are required to report there on arrival; the modern timber staging immediately upstream of the Office has been provided for this purpose, and arrival near slack water is much the easiest; upstream, there is also a narrow entrance to some limited berthing behind the staging. The Office will give berthing directions, collect harbour dues and berthing fees, and issue the useful 'Mariners' Guide to Rye' together with a copy of the harbour bye-laws and the security code to the WC/shower. Visiting arrivals out of hours should use a temporary berth before reporting in the next morning; however, it is anyway unwise for night arrivals to proceed further in the absence of local knowledge.

The choice of berthing at Rye is limited. The staging upstream of the Office has WC/shower facilities nearby [code from Harbour Office]; it is useful to those, including fishing vessels, who wish to take an early morning tide, but this is an isolated outpost a couple of miles from the town, and the river bed alongside dries to a hard bottom. The staging beneath the harbour office is reserved to the Harbour Master.

On the west bank opposite is the village of Rye Harbour, with dinghy sailing club, PH, cafe, and the lifeboat station; the jetty is unavailable for landing. The small craft berths here are soon to be removed to facilitate turning for commercial vessels, and there is no

THE QUAY AT RYE HARBOUR

provision for visitors. The Town Quay here is covered at HWS, and is available only for a short stay.

The channel upstream from the Harbour Office is marked by beacons on the stbd hand, together with some buoyage. On that hand, and particularly above *No 15* and *No 32*, the land floods extensively and a little care needs to be taken to be sure of remaining in the channel; behind the beacons, the water should never be regarded as navigable.

The continuation upstream passes Simmons Wharf on the port hand, where the fishing fleet is concentrated, and thence to the New Road bridge with an air draft of about 2.8m and the river bed at about CD. Above the bridge, the river passes through a rural setting with a small sluice on the stbd hand at 0.7nM, until the 'Scots Float Sluice' and lock is gained at 1.1nM.

RYE – THE ENTRANCE TO ROCK CHANNEL AT LW

Above the lock, the river is navigable for another 10nM or so to Bodiham, with a maintained depth of 3m, and an air draught of about 2m at the intermediate road bridges. There is a seasonal river bus between Bodiham and Rye.

THE RIVER BREDE MOORINGS and the turn for Strand Quay

Returning to the visitor berthing at the town, which is situated principally at Strand Quay, the approach is via Rock Channel. At 1nM upstream from the HM office, the uninspiring entrance to the channel will be found on the port hand, and is marked by the buoys Nos *44 [QR]* and 29 *[QG]*; the turn is tight, but identification is assisted by a signboard and arrow on the stbd bank, and a pair of buoys [*R* and *G*, *unlit*] marking the centre of the river channel which here is narrow.

On the stbd hand there is a succession of mud berths, with berthing end-on between piles; the better water is found nearer to these; they are maintained respectively by Rock Channel Marine, R&E, Moon Marine, Sandrock Marine, and a couple of further unnamed; these yards are primarily for long-term stay, but casual space may be available on prior enquiry; they provide few facilities.

Rock Channel is well buoyed on the port hand and runs reasonably true; at the commencement of the modern river wall on the stbd hand, the port hand buoys should be given a wide berth, as they mark a length of collapsed timber staging.

RYE – ROCK CHANNEL HAZARD AT LW

RYE – STRAND QUAY AT HW

RYE – STRAND QUAY AT LW

Immediately upstream is the commencement of the River Brede Moorings on the port hand, with the small basin of the sluice to the River Brede. The river here turns to stbd, and there is a notice on the bank directing visitors to Strand Quay.

At Strand Quay, there is a welcoming notice on the stbd hand immediately past the public slipway. Visitors are expected to berth on the town side [stbd hand on approach], but rafting up is not encouraged; at HW there is a stand of around 20mins, and there is adequate space for turning.

The Quay is about 200m in length, of steel piled whalings with fixed ladders every 15m, together with timber whalings and rings for mast strops, but fender boards are not provided.

The channel here dries to a trickle at chart datum, with the best water towards the downstream end; berthing is on soft clean mud, the banks of which rise 1m or more above the channel and have been dredged near level, but mast strops are still recommended for the first tide; a little thought is necessary to make best use of the spacing between the ladders and the power supply boxes. Long bow and stern lines are required to accommodate the rise and fall of around 3m, and fender boards should be watched for snagging.

The Quay can become crowded in season, and attracts overseas visitors; it is better to arrive early rather than late, notwithstanding having had to back the tide on reporting at the Harbour Master's office. The WC/shower [free of charge] is nearby in a single, tidily modern and comfortably sized family unit, adjoining the public conveniences; the tearoom profits from the inevitable waiting time, and a crew member needs to be posted as a lookout! The ambience is uniquely pleasant; berthing at the downstream end minimises nuisance from traffic noise and street lighting.

The seagulls are dire if attracted by titbits.

RYE — MARITIME INFORMATION

CHARTS Admiralty 1991, 5605, 536; Imray 2100

TIDAL DIFFERENCE Dover +0002
Tidal range 3 – 5m

WEATHER FORECASTS Available at Harbour Office

NAVIGATION AUTHORITY Environment Agency [as HM]

HARBOUR MASTER New Lydd Road, Camber
Rye Harbour Radio Ch 14 [225225]

SPEED LIMIT 6kts

BERTHING
Alongside drying berths at HM Office
but principally at Strand Quay
Both with shower/WC; water & elec at Strand Quay

YARDS [Rock Channel] All drying; few allocated to visitors, but some space usually available
Rock Channel Marine
storage ashore, on-board maintenance [223757]
R & E storage ashore [223234]
Moon Marine slip, general repairs, shower/WC [222679]
Sandrock Marine [226175]
Gary Fox water & elec; slip; limited storage ashore; onboard maintenance available [*07767* 217517]
River Brede Moorings
crane, storage ashore, general repairs [226213]

ENGINEERS
Mechanical Moon Marine, Rock Channel
Electronic Sussex Fishing Services, Rye [223895]

FUEL P&D from garage

SAILS and RIGGING
Northrop Sails, Ramsgate [*01843* 851665]

STD CODE 01797 ***unless shown otherwise***

RYE — TOWN INFORMATION

TRANSPORT
Rail [via Lewes or Ashford/London]
Buses The Wave [Stagecoach] [via Hastings or Dover]
Taxis A2B [*07752* 959795]; Rother Taxis [224554]; Tollgate [230630]

HOSPITAL
The William Harvey, Ashford [*01233* 633331]

DOCTOR
Rye Medical Centre, Kiln Drive, Rye Foreign [223333]

DENTIST
P. Davies, 6 East St., Rye [222834]

POLICE
Cinque Ports Street [not 24hrs]
Non emergency [101]

INFORMATION CENTRE
Heritage Centre, The Strand [226696]
www.heritagectre@btconnect.com

LIBRARY [Internet access]
High Street [*03456* 080196]

MUSEUM
Castle Museum, Ypres Tower

SHOPPING
Good general shopping, but scattered.
Supermarket opposite railway station

PUBS and RESTAURANTS
Wide choice, but many restaurants closed Sun / Mon.

STD CODE 01797 ***unless shown otherwise***

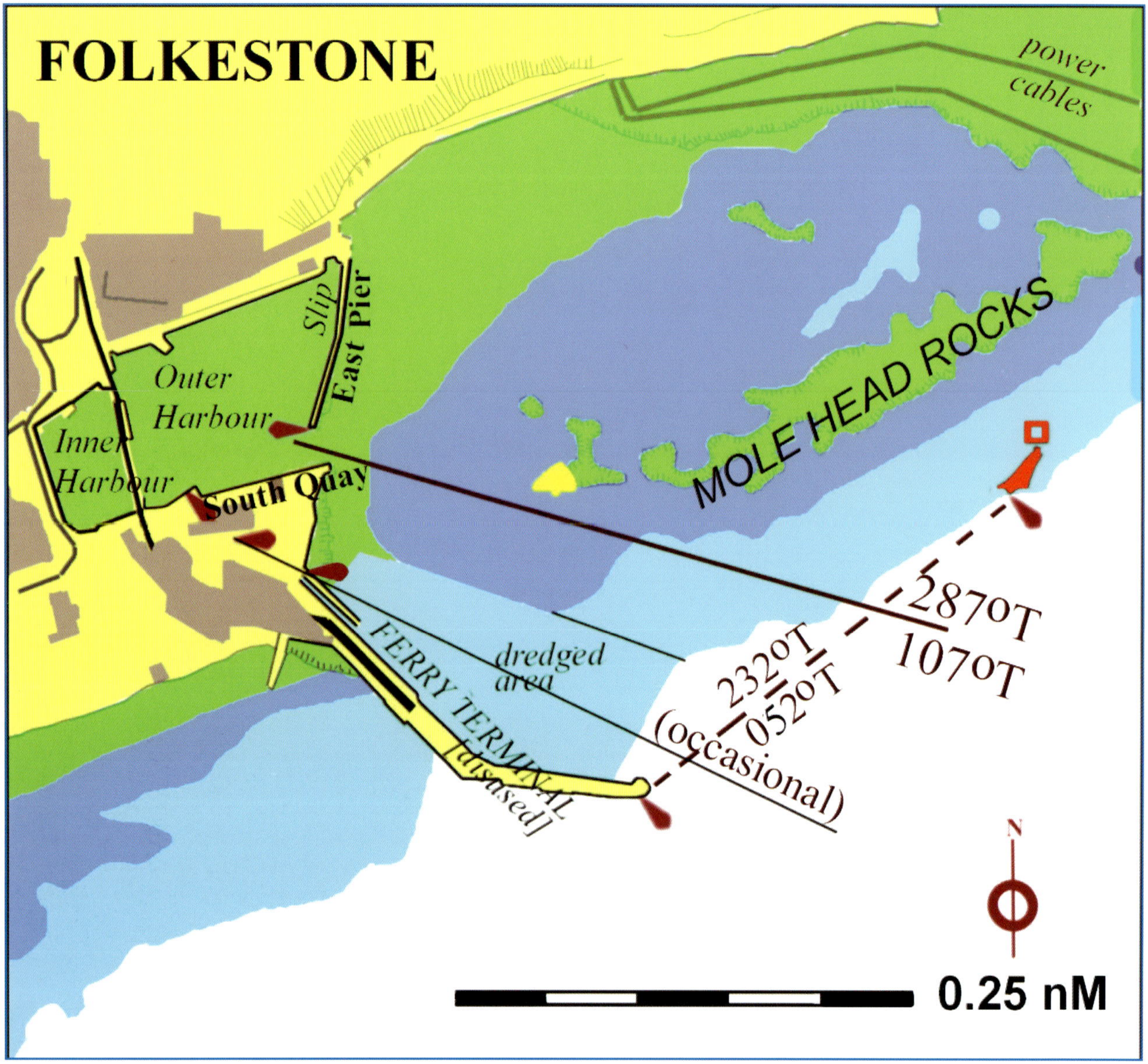

FOLKESTONE HARBOUR

The South

FOLKESTONE

Folkestone –'Folston' in early days – came into prominence when it was the base for the navy of King John, but only really expanded with Victorian holidays and the growth of cross-channel leisure traffic. The modern quay, outside the main harbour, has been largely abandoned since commercial operations were transferred to Dover in 2001. There is a generous modern town centre a few minutes from the harbour and there are pleasant coastal attractions but, apart from a colourful area adjoining the harbour, there is little of immediate interest.

FOLKESTONE AT AROUND 1900

FOLKESTONE HARBOUR AT LWN+1½

Navigation and Berthing

The entrance to this small drying harbour is guarded by the shoaling Mole Head outcrops, drying 1.2m; the approach track needs to be adopted with care, with entry restricted to about HW +/-1. The entrance, between the bulk of the South Quay and the East Pier *[QG]*, is about 30m in width with the best water at about mid-point, with an approach on 232°T maintaining the entrance just open, leaving the yellow buoy *[unlit]* at about 20m to stbd. In uncertain conditions, the final approach should be made from the point at which the vessel is in transit between the commercial pierhead *[Fl(2)10s]* and the red buoy *[FlR 5s]* marking the sewer outfall. The traffic signals at the pierhead [if in use] are to be obeyed.

An informal approach is by following inshore at about a boat's length off, the east side of the commercial pier until the head of the old RoRo terminal is reached, before turning due N until the harbour entrance is fully open, thus keeping clear of the outcrop beneath the wall; a sharp lookout needs to be kept for small craft leaving the harbour. There are no really useful leading marks, although there is a conspicuous hotel at the western end of the Inner Harbour, and the cupola topped flats are readily seen; the leading lights off the old RoRo ferry terminal are only occasional. The commercial pier infrequently receives commercial vessels, but is no longer in use as a ferry terminal.

FOLKESTONE HARBOUR AT 1nM OFF

Within the breakwaters, there are the outer and inner harbours separated by the railway viaduct; the swing bridge in the viaduct has not been in operation since the cessation of the ferry service.

The outer harbour is well protected, and the bottom of mud and sand shelves gently. There are numerous mooring buoys and ground tackle, both for yachts and for fishing vessels; all are allocated and there is no provision for visitors.

A short-term berth may be available on application to either the Harbour Master [VHF Ch 15, 16 / 01303 254597], or to the Folkestone Y & MB Club which controls many of the moorings near the viaduct. An alongside berth on the South Quay is feasible, but there are few ladders, fender boards are needed, it is difficult to accommodate the tidal range of up to 5m, and the bottom is foul in parts.

Anchorage within the harbour risks being intrusive and also fouling the extensive ground tackle. There may be temporary space at the foot of the slipway in the north-east corner, in the shelter of the East Pier, where there is good holding in sand; this dries to about 3.7m.

The Inner Harbour is available to small craft on long-term stay, but also for landing. The access is through the viaduct arches; with the best water at the arch nearest the pier, where there are about 3m between the sea bed and the top of the arch; the sea bed there is at about 2m above CD.

YACHT MOORINGS AT HW with the viaduct behind

FOLKESTONE	MARITIME INFORMATION
CHARTS	Admiralty 1698, 1991, SC5605 Imray C8, 2100.5
TIDAL DIFFERENCE	Dover -0010
NAVIGATION AUTHORITY	Folkestone Harbour Company [240400]
PORT CONTROL	'Folkestone Port Control' Ch 15 [714354]
YACHT CLUB	Folkestone Y&MBC North Street [251754]
BERTHING	Anchorage in Harbour, or occasional mooring via YC [*01304* 201525]
FUEL	P&D from garage
FACILITIES	See Dover / Ramsgate

STD CODE 01303 *unless shown otherwise*

FOLKESTONE	TOWN INFORMATION
TRANSPORT	
Rail	[Dover/London]
Buses	Stagecoach [via Hastings or Dover]
Taxis:	Channel Cars [252252]; Folkestone Taxis [252000]
HOSPITAL	The William Harvey, Ashford [*01233* 633331]
POLICE	Bouverie Road West [not 24hrs] Non emergency [101]
INFORMATION CENTRE	Harbour Street www.discoverfolkestone.co.uk
LIBRARY [Internet access] and MUSEUM	Grace Hill [850123]
SHOPPING	Good general shopping in town centre [$^1/_2$M]
PUBS and RESTAURANTS	Limited choice, but the area above the North Quay is colourful
ENTERTAINMENT	Cinema [221230]

STD CODE 01303 *unless shown otherwise*

YACHT MOORINGS AT LW

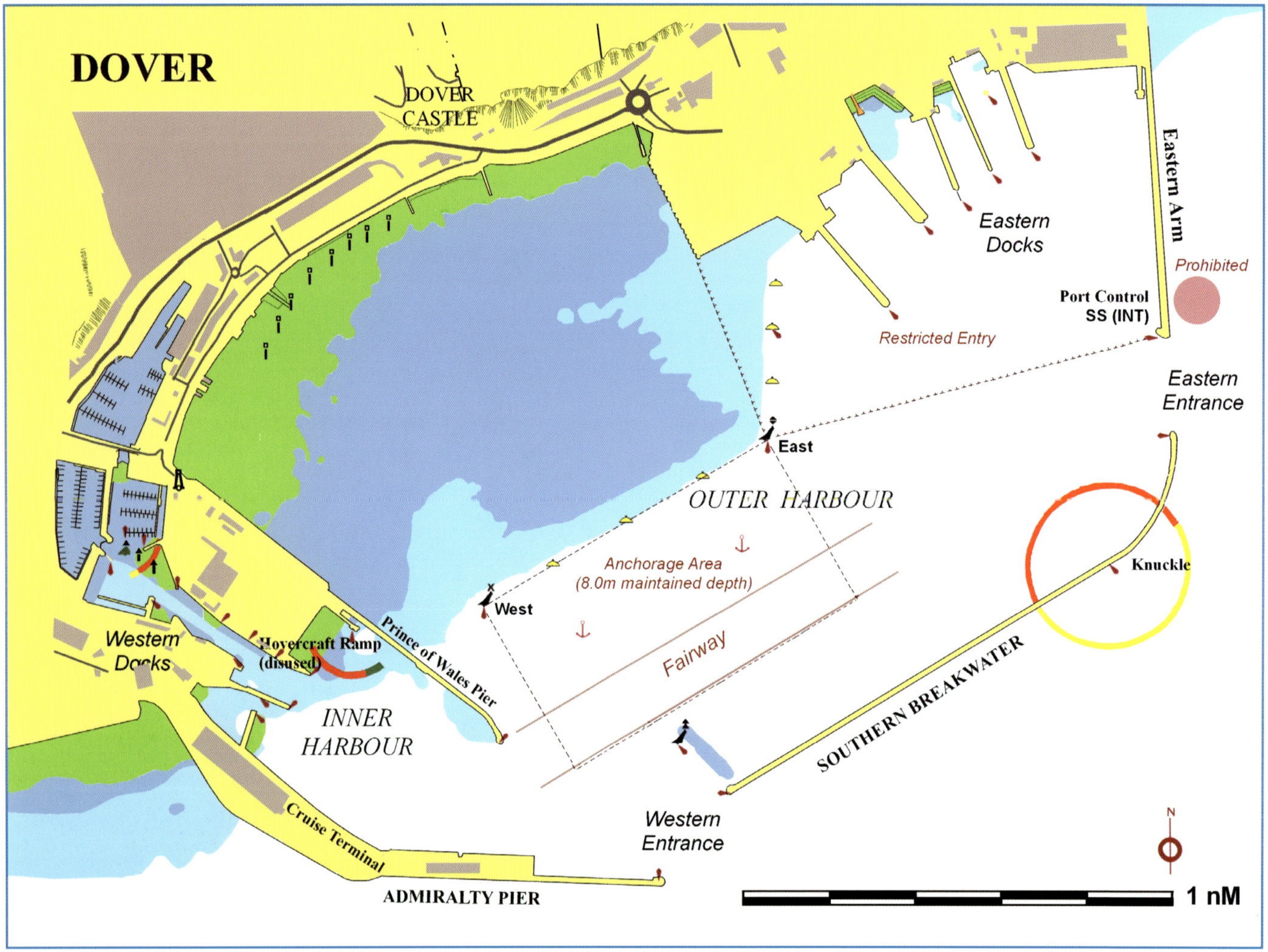

DOVER HARBOUR

The South

DOVER

Dover is Port and Castle at England's 'Gateway to Europe' and, in this sense, it has remained unchanged since the Bronze Age; indeed, here is the earliest excavated sea-going boat in the world. The town is one of contrasts between its efficient port, marina and outstanding attractions, and a hillside town centre whose potential charm was abandoned to appalling piecemeal redevelopment.

The yachtsman entering this busy port in a professional manner is met with helpful courtesy. A full day's stopover is inadequate to take on board the principal attractions; the town centre is a good half-mile from the marina, but the marina will one day be redeveloped on a site within the bay.

DOVER BEACH and WATERLOO CRESCENT

DOVER CASTLE

DOVER HARBOUR WESTERN ENTRANCE at LWN+1½

Navigation and Berthing

The Dover Straits are the busiest shipping lane in the world, and Dover Harbour is about the busiest in the United Kingdom, and there is not a lot of scope for manoeuvre by the ferries trying to maintain a timetable; their acceleration from the port, and the speed of approaching 'Fast Ferries', should not be underestimated.

Many yachtsmen view Dover with trepidation, but this is unnecessary given a watchful eye, a well-found boat, and a preparedness to follow the published pilotage information and the clear instructions on VHF from Port Control. Comfort can be taken from the highly professional service, which probably has visiting yachts on radar long before they are likely to cause a problem, and which has fast escort boats at the ready; incidents in the vicinity of the port are very rare indeed [but incidents between the ferries manoeuvring within the harbour are not so uncommon!]. The cardinal sin is a failure to make - and maintain - contact with Port Control.

DOVER HARBOUR

DOVER HARBOUR EASTERN ENTRANCE at LWN+1½

A night-time entry is perfectly feasible. Entry under sail should not be attempted other than in an emergency, and even then only with the cognisance of Port Control who will probably despatch an escort. The useful Dover Marina Visitors' Guide is obtainable by post from the marina [Dover Marina, Dover, Kent CT17 9TF, tel. 01304 241663].

The approach from the west is from Dungeness, which is only 3nM from the westbound shipping lane, and also passes the Firing Practice Ranges off Hythe. The passage therefore, will always be via the inshore traffic zone on a course of about 048°T, to the small craft holding area at 200m off the western entrance; from close inshore, the only light visible may be that on the nearer arm of the entrance *[Fl 7.5s]*.

DOVER HARBOUR - THE APPROACHES to the MARINAS

Dover Port Control on Ch **74**, 12 or 16 should be advised of entry intentions at about 1nM off; there will be a requirement to report again when at 200m off; if there is single-handed difficulty with the VHF, that too should be made clear. There may well be an instruction to wait for commercial vessels entering or leaving; this may take perhaps fifteen or twenty minutes, in what can be the very uncomfortable conditions of a confused sea, and it is better therefore to furl sails earlier rather than later. There are also the conventional IPT signals *[RRR/GWG]* on the seaward end of the Admiralty Pier.

The entrance should be made at about midway between the two arms *[Fl 7.5s* and *OcR 30s]*. On entering, there may be strong cross-tides and a heavy swell but, once inside, the shelter of the wall is a welcome relief; additional care is necessary when tidal heights are below 2m. Initially at least, the centre of the approach channel to the Western Docks should be held, being watchful for any commercial traffic in the vicinity.

DOVER HARBOUR – THE TIDAL BASIN

In either case, berthing is side-on to pontoon fingers with adequate cleats; the marina office is situated between the Tidal Basin and the Granville Dock, near the swing bridge to the Wellington Dock, and is open 24hrs; a courtesy pack and security code will be issued on reporting in.

The Wellington Dock is accessed *via* the lock beneath the swing bridge. It is open for about HW +/- 1 ½, and it is mostly for longer-stay vessels, for which it is a little cheaper.

On departure, permission is again needed from Dover Port Control. If leaving the marina, liaison with the marina office is appropriate, and permission from Port Control should be requested when the old Hoverspeed ramp is abeam, and stating the entrance being made for; if leaving the anchorage, permission should be sought as soon as way is being made; a departure via the eastern entrance may entail a wait adjoining the Knuckle on the Southern Breakwater. It should also be borne in mind that sea conditions outside the harbour will be substantially more severe than inside.

A passage past the port should be made standing reasonably well off to maintain a good lookout for potential traffic at the entrances. It does no harm to contact Dover Port Control to advise them of intentions, and to request advice as to imminent departures or arrivals. At first sight, there is a lot of detail to assimilate, but this is only a prompt properly to prepare the passage plan; given this, the port presents no great difficulties to the visiting yachtsman, and such a plan will be invaluable at times of restricted visibility.

The approach from the east is similarly via the inshore traffic zone, but observing that the Goodwin Sands are within 2nM of South Foreland. From the South Foreland, standing off a mile or so is a more comfortable avoidance of the beam seas on the final approach. The entry procedure is as from the west; Port Control endeavours to give clearance to yachts ahead of an incoming ferry, but this leaves the possibility of having to abort with a starboard [inshore] turn; it may be necessary also to wait for departing traffic, but waiting outside the eastern entrance inshore usually is not nearly as uncomfortable as at the western. The landmark will be the Port Control tower on the Eastern Arm, and there are IPT signals there also. Entrance should be made midway between the two arms *[FlR 2.5s* and *FlG 5s]*.

Ahead, is a reception pontoon for use by those who have been unable to make contact with the marina; the entrance to Granville Dock is to the left of this, and there is a depth restriction at the sill.

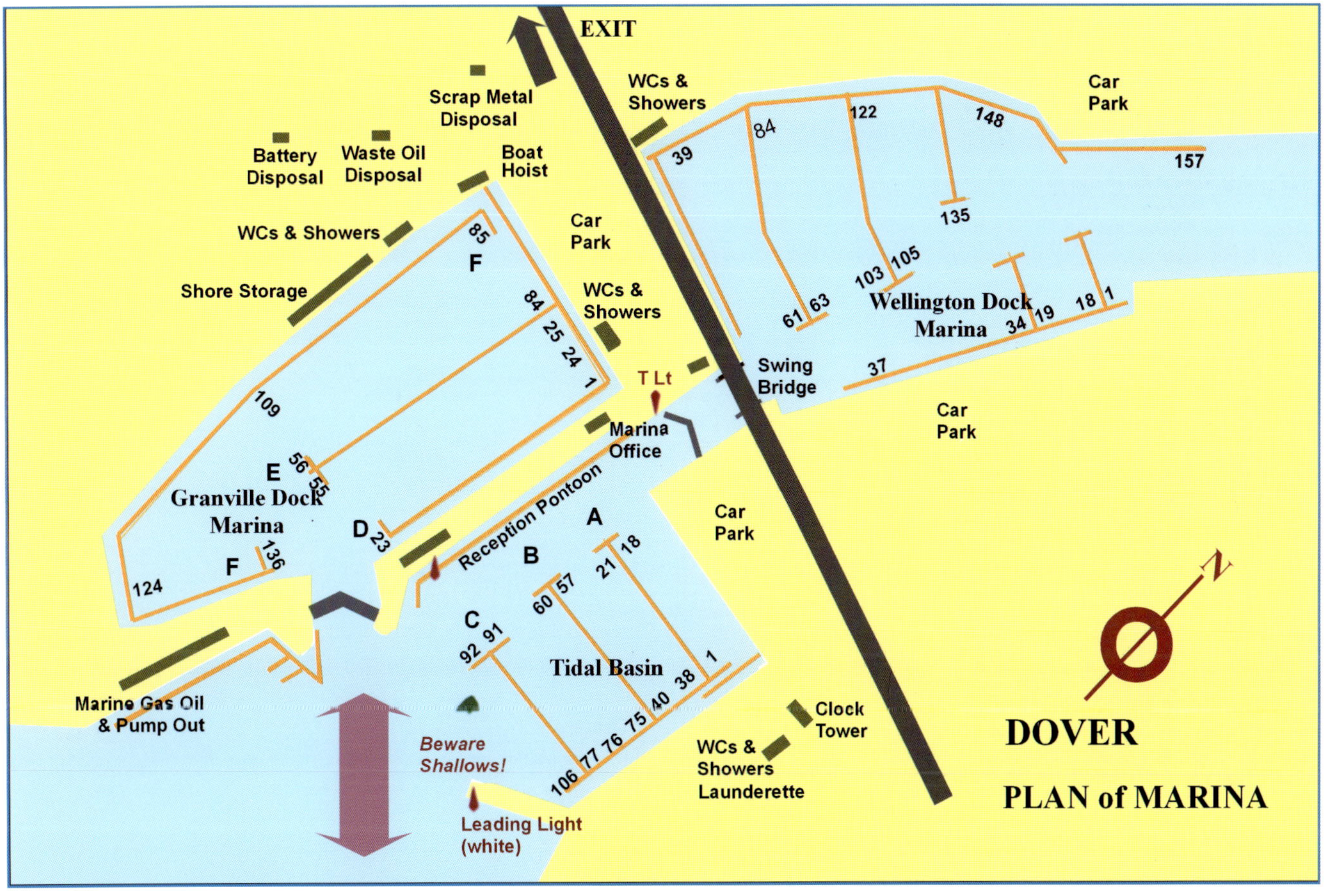

DOVER HARBOUR – THE MARINAS Courtesy Dover Harbour Board [adapted]

DOVER — MARITIME INFORMATION

CHARTS Admiralty 1098, 1828, SC 505
Imray C8, 2100.5

WEATHER FORECASTS Posted at Marina Office

NAVIGATION AUTHORITY & HM
Dover Harbour Board [24hr] [240400]

PORT CONTROL
Dover Port Control Ch 12, 16, 74 [206063]

YACHT CLUB
Royal Cinque Ports YC Waterloo Crescent [206262]
Terrace & Bar, occas. Food, WC/Shwrs

BERTHING Anchorage in bay [advise Port Control]
Dover Marina: Shwrs/WCs, water, elec, launderettes
Tidal Basin [all-tide] 106 berths, max 24hrs
Wellington Dock [HW +/- 11/2hrs] 157 berths
Granville Dock [HW +/- 4hrs] 136 berths

FUEL Crosswell Quay [adj lock] [Gas Oil]
P & D in cans from garage

PUMP-OUT Crosswell Quay

MAINTENANCE
General M&P Marine Services [*07854* 904380]
[including some M & E]
Mech Coastal Rides [201073]
[including some general]
Electronic Positive Marine Electrical
[Ramsgate] [*07770* 382980]

CHANDLER Sharpe & Enright, Snargate St.
Calor & Gas

SAILS & RIGGING See Ramsgate

STD CODE 01304 ***unless shown otherwise***

DOVER — TOWN INFORMATION

TRANSPORT
Rail [Dover Priory] [North Kent service for London]
Buses Stagecoach [for Hastings to west, or London]
Taxis Rother Cars [224554] Tollgate [230630]

HOSPITAL
The William Harvey, Ashford [*01233* 633331]

POLICE Ladywell [not 24hrs]
Non emergency [101]

INFORMATION CENTRE
Market Square [201066]

LIBRARY [Internet access]
Market Square [204311]

MUSEUM
Market Square [201066]

SHOPPING
Good general shopping

PUBS
Numerous, but unexciting

RESTAURANTS
Limited choice [many close Mondays]

ENTERTAINMENT
Leisure Centre, Townwall Street [201145]
Cinema, Gaol Lane [adj Info Centre] [228000]

EVENTS
Town Pageant [Spring Bank Holiday]
Dover Carnival [First Sat. in July]
Dover Regatta [Mid-July]

STD CODE 01304 ***unless shown otherwise***

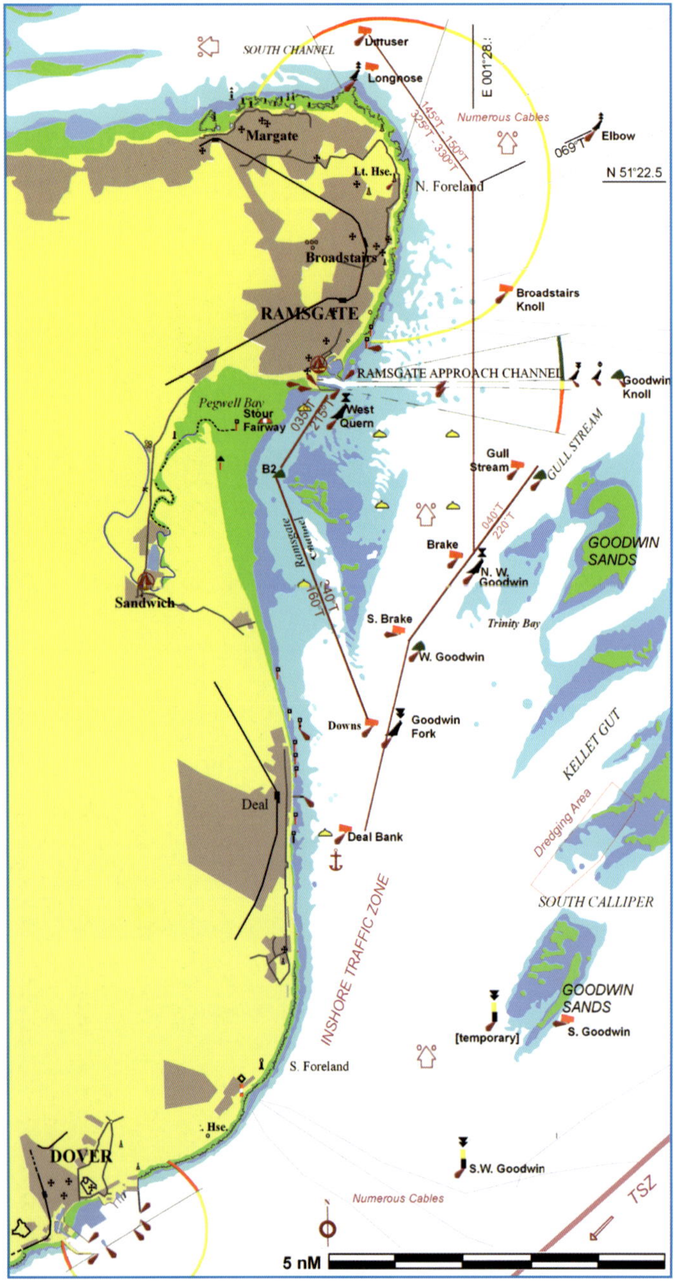
SOUTH CHANNEL
Diffuser
Longnose
E 001°28.
Numerous Cables
145°T - 150°T
325°T - 330°T
Elbow
069°T
Margate
Lt. Hse.
N. Foreland
N 51°22.5
Broadstairs
Broadstairs Knoll
RAMSGATE
RAMSGATE APPROACH CHANNEL
Goodwin Knoll
Pegwell Bay
Stour Fairway
West Quern
035°T
215°T
B2
Gull Stream
GULL STREAM
040°T
220°T
Brake
GOODWIN SANDS
N. W. Goodwin
Ramsgate Channel
Sandwich
Trinity Bay
S. Brake
W. Goodwin
Downs
Goodwin Fork
KELLET GUT
Deal
Deal Bank
Dredging Area
SOUTH CALLIPER
INSHORE TRAFFIC ZONE
GOODWIN SANDS
[temporary]
S. Goodwin
S. Foreland
Hse.
DOVER
S.W. Goodwin
Numerous Cables
TSZ
5 nM

The Forelands

OVERVIEW

The waters from Dover to North Foreland, coloured by centuries of history, comprise a mere two miles' wide channel between the mainland and the notorious Goodwin Sands, and extend some fifteen miles from south to north; in this section are included Sandwich, Ramsgate and Broadstairs. The cross-channel traffic from Dover is frequent, runs predominantly east-west; there is an infrequent service which initially adopts a more northerly [inshore] route. The traffic otherwise is light, but includes pilot and work boats, as well as those of inshore fishing fleets.

East of South Foreland there is some shelter from the prevailing south-westerlies, but there is a long fetch and seas may be steep; inshore, the sea bed is mostly sandy shingle with variable holding, and strong easterlies produce very untidy conditions. Dover and Ramsgate both provide all-tide access and good shelter. There is a good, and historically important, anchorage just off the northern end of Deal with good holding in sand or mud, but there are patches of shingle with poor holding; there is a shallow anchorage in the Ramsgate Channel [Pegwell Bay] with good holding in sand, but this is not recommended with the wind from the east or south-east; an anchor ball or riding light should be shown in all these areas. Some shelter may be found in the lee of Folkestone Pier, but subject to surge.

Weather

The weather, in comparison with that of the south Kentish coast, is more influenced by that of the continental mainland; conditions are therefore a little less predictable. The increased probability of cold north-easterly airstreams meeting those of the moist and warmer Atlantic, is conducive to fog. The straits channel the winds somewhat, and can give rise to steep seas.

Tides

The tidal streams follow the coastline, and are strongly influenced by the confluence with those of the North Sea. At Dover HW+3, the tide is making from the east but still on the ebb from Dover; these streams meet at Dungeness and are deflected towards CS3, and slow-moving craft should be aware of this.

The stand then moves eastwards to a little east of Dover at Dover HW; the east flowing ebb continues to slack water at North Foreland at HW Dover +5. The tidal streams between Dover and North Foreland run at up to 2.3kts in both directions; planning is necessary to pass North Foreland in comfort – if at all under sail.

Comfortable passage making is highly dependent on playing the tides, not forgetting the significant tidal differences among The Swale, The Medway and The Thames.

THE FORELANDS	MARITIME INFORMATION
CHARTS	Admiralty SC5605.2, 8, 9; SC5606.4 Imray 2100.5
TIDAL DIFFERENCES [approx] on Dover	Sandwich +0025; Ramsgate +0030 Broadstairs +0037; Sheerness +0130
COASTGUARD	Dover Ch 69 16, 80 [01304 210008]
HARBOUR MASTERS	Dover [Port Control] Ch 69, 16, 80 [01304 210008] Sandwich [07958 376183] Ramsgate [Port Control] Ch14 [01843 572112] Broadstairs [01843 861879]

SOUTH OVERVIEW	WAYPOINTS
Dover Western Ent. [mid]	51°06’.7N; 001°19’.7E
Dover Eastern Ent [mid]	51°07’.2N; 001°20.5E
Downs / Goodwin Fork [midway, approx.]	51)14’.4N; 001°25’.6E
South Brake / West Goodwin [midway, approx.]	51°15’.6N; 001°27’.2E
Brake / North West Goodwin [midway, approx.]	51°16’.7N; 001°29’.9E
Stour Fairway [seasonal, & subject to relocation]	51°18’.9N; 001°23’.5E
West Quern	51°19’.0N; 001°25’.5E
Ramsgate [Approach Channel]	51°19.5N
Broadstairs [Pierhead]	51°21’.5N; 001°26’.8E
Margate Diffuser	51°24’.6N; 001°26’.0E

Dover to North Foreland

At risk of repetition, awareness of cross-channel traffic at Dover is restated, and a passage past Dover should be made near a mile off to give maximum visibility of traffic, both inbound and outbound; once past Dover, an inshore passage is recommended.

A northbound passage from Dover Harbour will almost invariably commence from the eastern entrance; an inshore passage is recommended by Port Control to avoid a possible encounter with traffic – but the closer inshore, the more uncomfortable the beam seas.

The coastline here is of chalk cliffs, which continue around South Foreland. On the hill about 2 cables east of Dover are the radio masts; at about 4 cables is the old lighthouse on the cliff top, and to the east of this is the Dover Memorial. There are rare, but unpredictable, substantial rock falls; it is safer therefore not to close too much inshore.

From South Foreland the cliffs and shoreline rocks diminish progressively, running due north into narrow sandy beaches, with an allocated swimming area at Kingsdown, and the landmarks of radio mast and church behind. Walmer Castle is behind, but not readily visible from, the beach. Deal castle is just off the beach, with the landmarks of water tower and pier with ‘T’ head *[2 Fl*

Walmer Castle, one of Henry VIII’s coastal fortifications, is the official residence of the Lord Warden of the Cinque Ports. It is not now readily visible from the sea.

R]; a lifeboat is anchored off, but the security gate above the ladder precludes casual landing.

The coastline from here to Ramsgate is progressively low-lying with the extensive sand banks running into the historic Pegwell Bay.

The northbound passage from Deal offers the choice of that *via* the Ramsgate Channel, or offshore into the Gull Stream deep water channel. The two routes are separated by The Brake, an irregular area of drying sand banks prone to shifting.

The inshore Ramsgate Channel is slightly the shorter for entry to Ramsgate, and leads directly into the Ramsgate Harbour small craft holding area [south]; it is also the obvious approach from the south for Pegwell Bay and the R. Stour for Sandwich. The channel has a minimum charted depth of 2m, but the only buoyage is *B2 [G, unlit]* marking the northwest extremity of the drying shoals; the channel is therefore unsuitable for a night passage without familiarity, and there is little light scatter from the land.

The offshore passage will be made from between *Downs* and *Goodwin Fork* for *W Goodwin [FlG 5s]* on a course of about 040° T [220° T] to the west cardinal *NW Goodwin [Q9 15s]*, and commercial traffic will have followed this course for the Gull Stream. It is usually convenient simply to head north from *NW Goodwin*, leaving to port the seasonal buoys *[Y, unlit]*, for the Ramsgate Approach which is well buoyed. The west cardinal *West Quern [YBY, Fl6, LFl]* is to be treated with respect.

In the area between The Brake and Ramsgate Harbour, there are several lit buoys; these mark shifting sand banks, and the buoyage is always open to revision; it is therefore unwise simply to rely on the GPS for a precise course. At night time, and when approaching from the south, identification of the buoys can be difficult when they are in transit and against the backdrop of shore lights; an enlarged and marked copy of a chart extract is invaluable and, if confusion continues, a certain solution is in holding offshore until the Ramsgate Approach Channel is identified.

THE DOVER MEMORIAL

WALMER CASTLE

THE DEAL TIME BALL and MUSEUM - The tower is about 200m south of the pier.

The Goodwin Sands may be explored from Trinity Bay. This should be attempted only under ideal conditions, and certainly avoided if there are strong easterlies. There must be an awareness of uncharted changing depths and numerous wrecks, both on and around the sand banks, and in Trinity Bay itself. A northerly passage, if required, should be via Kellett Gut or the Gull Stream, the latter being in use by commercial traffic. A passage to the east of the Goodwins is well enough buoyed, but *CS4 [Fl(4)Y 15s]* marks the TSZ. A turn inshore is best deferred until the approach channel has been gained.

The approach channel runs due east-west and is dredged. The entrance to Ramsgate Harbour will be made by following outside the channel to either the north or south holding area, pending entry permission from Port Control [Ch 14]; the use of the appropriate holding area also avoids the need to cross the approach channel on entry.

The preferred crossing of the approach

The Deal tower was originally a semaphore station, and was replaced by the present time ball in 1855; it was a time signal for the naval ships at anchor.

NORTH FORELAND at LWN +1.

channel, for small craft on an inshore passage, is immediately to the east of the north cardinal *North Quern* [which also means exactly as intended]. About a half-mile north of Ramsgate is the conspicuous Granville Hotel, followed by a cliff-top house with tower, and the small bay of Dumpton Gap with its sandy beach. Broadstairs is a small bay beneath the cliffs with the town above, and a drying harbour partly enclosed by its pier *[2FlR (vert)]* and adjacent concrete groyne *[QR]*.

The coastline beyond Ramsgate is progressively steeper-to beneath chalk cliffs; there are shoaling patches which, from a half-mile off, provide a minimum charted depth of 4m, but the Broadstairs Knolls can produce some untidy conditions around low water. The inshore track is used by fast pilot boats and fishing vessels, and there are numerous lobster pots.

The northbound passage continues on the track from *NW Goodwin*, until the North Foreland lighthouse bears 270°T or less, and when the north cardinal *Elbow* bears about 069°T. It is then safe to turn on to between 325°T - 330°T for the buoy *[FlR 5s]* marking the Margate outfall, so as to clear the Longnose Ledge; in daytime, this buoy is not to be confused with that inshore *[R, unlit]*; care also should be taken to avoid the tidal set onto the ledge, which is deceptively extensive – note the currents around the headland.

The North Foreland lighthouse, of 42m ht, is more for the benefit of commercial traffic than small craft, although useful in taking bearings; the light is exhibited at night-time only. These details are to assist a night passage, and are generally unnecessary for small craft in good daylight when the shoreline may be hugged more closely.

NORTH FORELAND LIGHTHOUSE

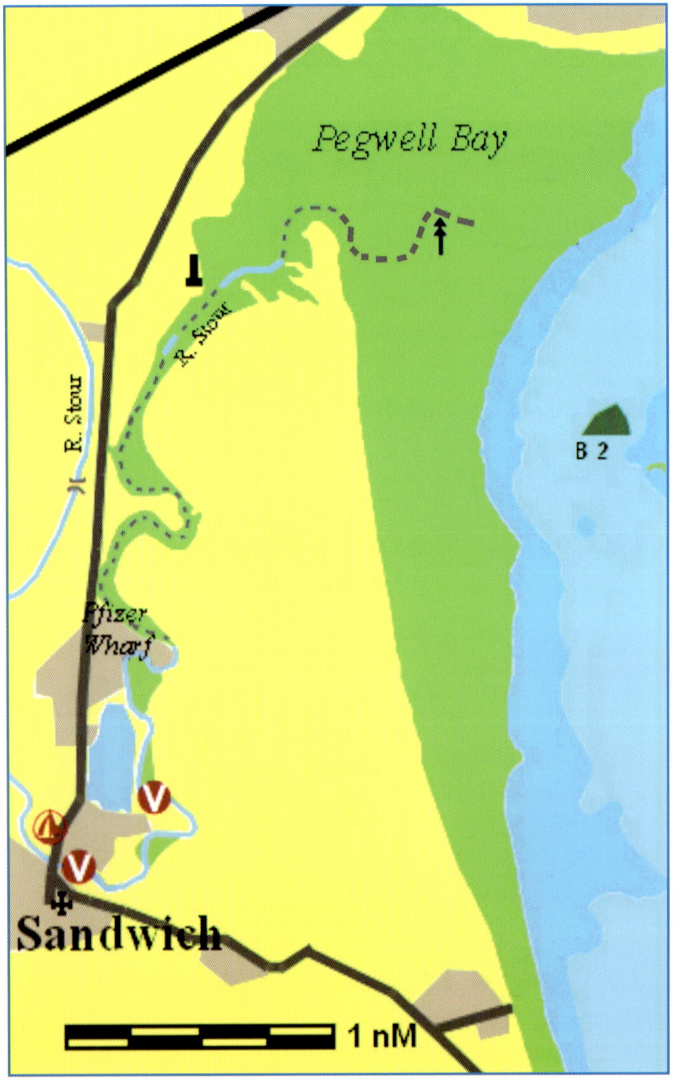

PEGWELL BAY AND THE RIVER STOUR

The Forelands

SANDWICH

Sandwich, another of the Cinque Ports, was in medieval times the premier port of the country, and its history drips from the eaves and oozes from every crack in the pavements; the layout of the small and delightfully confusing central area has changed little, but it still manages to be actively attractive and hospitable. The town is busy in the summer season, but there is no undue emphasis on tourism.

The navigation for a visiting yachtsman is unchallenging. The public berthing at the Town Quay was, for many years, abysmal; the Quay is now under full reconstruction as a part of improved flood defences, and visitor berthing was resumed in August 2014 with some improvements.

SANDWICH – THE GUILDHALL

SANDWICH – QUAY LANE and FISHERGATE

Sandwich was, for centuries, the major port in England - long before London was of significance. It enjoyed access to the Wantsum Channel, running from Pegwell Bay northwards to Reculver; this provided a sheltered passage avoiding the North Foreland, and it was at the nearby Richborough that the Romans established their bridgehead.

Navigation and Berthing

The entrance to the River Stour is from Pegwell Bay, where there is little water and possibly insufficient on some neaps; following the demolition of the chimney and cooling towers of Richborough power station, and the discontinuance of both the safe water mark *Stour Fairway* and the leading boards on the beach, a local chart is essential; entry should not be attempted in heavy weather, or in poor visibility, without good familiarity.

The river bed is more a depression in the flats than a defined channel; its course changes frequently – in parts by as much as 50m in a season – as influenced by strong winds and river flood conditions.

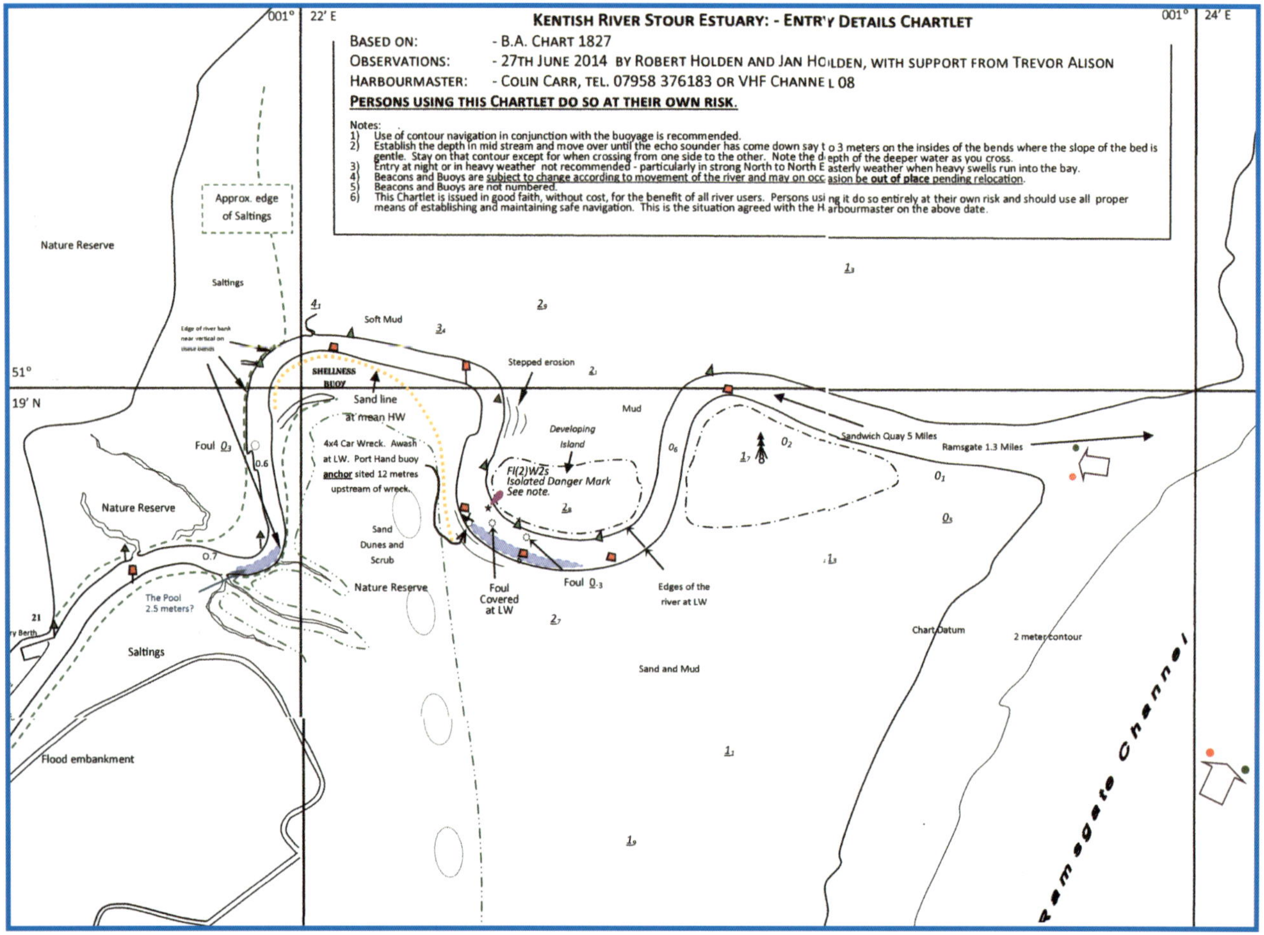

THE ENTRANCE TO THE RIVER STOUR [2014] [Adapted from © R Holden 2014]

The location of 'Stour Fairway' used to be assisted by a transit on the cooling towers of Richborough power station, but these were demolished in the spring of 2012.

THE ENTRANCE TO THE RIVER STOUR at LWN+1.
The entrance is navigable at HWN+1.

THE R. STOUR – SANDWICH MARINA

A perennial debt of gratitude is owed to Robert Holden, of the Sandwich S&MBC, who undertakes – and publishes - an annual survey; this is freely available *via* www.highwaymarine.co.uk – but even so it is sensible to check with Highway Marine [01304 614814] or the Harbour Master [07958 376183] for the latest advice.

There has recently been placed an additional port hand buoy ***Shellness** [unlit]* immediately north of Shellness point, marking a recently discovered historic wreck. This corner should not be cut, as the deeper water is to be found on the outside of the bend, the

SANDWICH – UPSTREAM BERTHING

SANDWICH – THE OLD TOWN QUAY at half-tide.
The Barbican Bridge is in the background.

channel having moved north over the winter of 2013-2014.

The depth upstream is mostly about 0.7m above CD; there is no buoyage, but the course is not difficult to find. It is best not to tuck too closely into the abandoned wharf and the cut above, and

At the entrance to the river, there is a colony of the 'Common Seal', around forty in number and growing; yachtsmen should avoid intrusion. The 'Common Seal' is actually less common than the 'Grey Seal', which has colonised the Goodwin Sands.

GROVEFERRY

FORDWYCH

then to favour the stbd hand until the Pfizer chemicals' wharf is reached; here, there is some shoaling immediately under the wharf. Pfizer are withdrawing from the site, which will be redeveloped.

There is a berthing and yard facility on the stbd hand *[Sandwich Marina]* with extensive shore storage and some facilities, but this is about a mile from the town centre and is not primarily for visitors. Above, the best water is to be found on the outside of the bends, and a lookout needs to be kept for overhanging trees.

The town berthing is either at the Town Quay or, upstream of the bridge, to that of Highway Marine. Sandwich is one of the few 'Free Ports', where there is a right of entry without notice, but notice to the Harbour Master is nevertheless appreciated.

The reconstructed Town Quay has been dredged near level, to about CD at the downstream end, and to about 1.4m above CD at the upstream end; the best position is probably about opposite the toilets' block; the upstream end should be left clear for the Harbour Master's boat, which is used also for excursions. The bottom is of clean mud, and mooring is to rings set onto the quayside, with occasional ladders; the shore facilities comprise a modern shower and WC block [office hours, and chargeable], and there is also a cold water tap.

The upstream berthing requires passage through the road bridge, which is opened to order. This operation is contracted out, but the quoted telephone number is changed frequently, and it is better to contact the Harbour Master; the service is available 24/7, but there is up to an hour's wait for the crew, who will not open the bridge until the vessel is seen to be under way.

The quayside berthing on the port hand is private, but it may soon become managed by Highway Marine.

On the right bank are pontoon berths accommodating craft of up to 25m; the depths vary between 1m at LWS and drying, but there is restricted availability for visitors; prior enquiry should be made of Highway Marine.

The river is navigable for a further 10nM to Fordwych, but masted craft should not proceed above Highway Marine because of low-level overhead power cables. River depths are subject to rainfall as much as to tide, but better than 1m will generally be found.

The air draft is restricted to about 2m at the road bridge at Grove Ferry, at about 5nM. There is a good riverside quay and PH there, as at the charming village of Fordwych. Fordwych was the medieval port for the building of Canterbury Cathedral; the upstream road bridge has an air draft of only 1m.

The outline of the medieval stone wharves is still visible beneath the garden walls abutting the river at Fordwych.

SANDWICH	MARITIME INFORMATION
CHARTS	Admiralty SC 5605.9; Imray 2100.5 See also, for 2014 local survey *www.highwaymarinegroup.co.uk*
TIDAL DIFFERENCE on Dover	+0015 [Richborough] +0100 [Town Quay]
NAVIGATION AUTHORITY	Sandwich Port and Haven Commissioners [617917]
HARBOUR MASTER	[*07958* 376183]
BRIDGE OPENING	[207707] [*07860* 378792 out of hours] or HM
BERTHING	**Town Quay** [Apply HM] alongside drying berths, WC/shower (not 24hrs)] **Highway Marine Ltd** [613925] Upstream, 70 tidal pontoon berths Crane to 10t, storage, general maintenance
YACHT CLUB	Sandwich S&MBC [617650]
YARDS	Highway Marine Ltd
CHANDLERS	Highway Marine Ltd Bosuns Locker, Ramsgate [Calor & Gaz]
ENGINEERS	
Mechanical	Highway Marine Service Centre [614814]
Electronic	Positive Marine Electronics [Ramsgate] [*07770* 382920]
FUEL	P&D from garage
SAILS and RIGGING	Northrop Sails, Ramsgate [*01843* 851665]

STD CODE 01304 ***unless shown otherwise***

SANDWICH	TOWN INFORMATION
TRANSPORT	
Rail	Sandwich [via Lewes or Ashford/London]
Buses	National Express
Taxis	AM Cars [614209] Sandwich Cars [617424]
HOSPITAL	The William Harvey, Ashford [*01233* 633331]
POLICE	Non emergency [101]
INFORMATION CENTRE	Guildhall [613565]
LIBRARY [Internet access]	Market Street
MUSEUM	Guildhall
SHOPPING	Adequate general shopping, but scattered Supermarket behind Guildhall
PUBS and RESTAURANTS	Limited choice, but more than adequate
CINEMA	Delf Street [620480]

STD CODE 01304 ***unless shown otherwise***

COMMON SEALS AT THE RIVER ENTRANCE

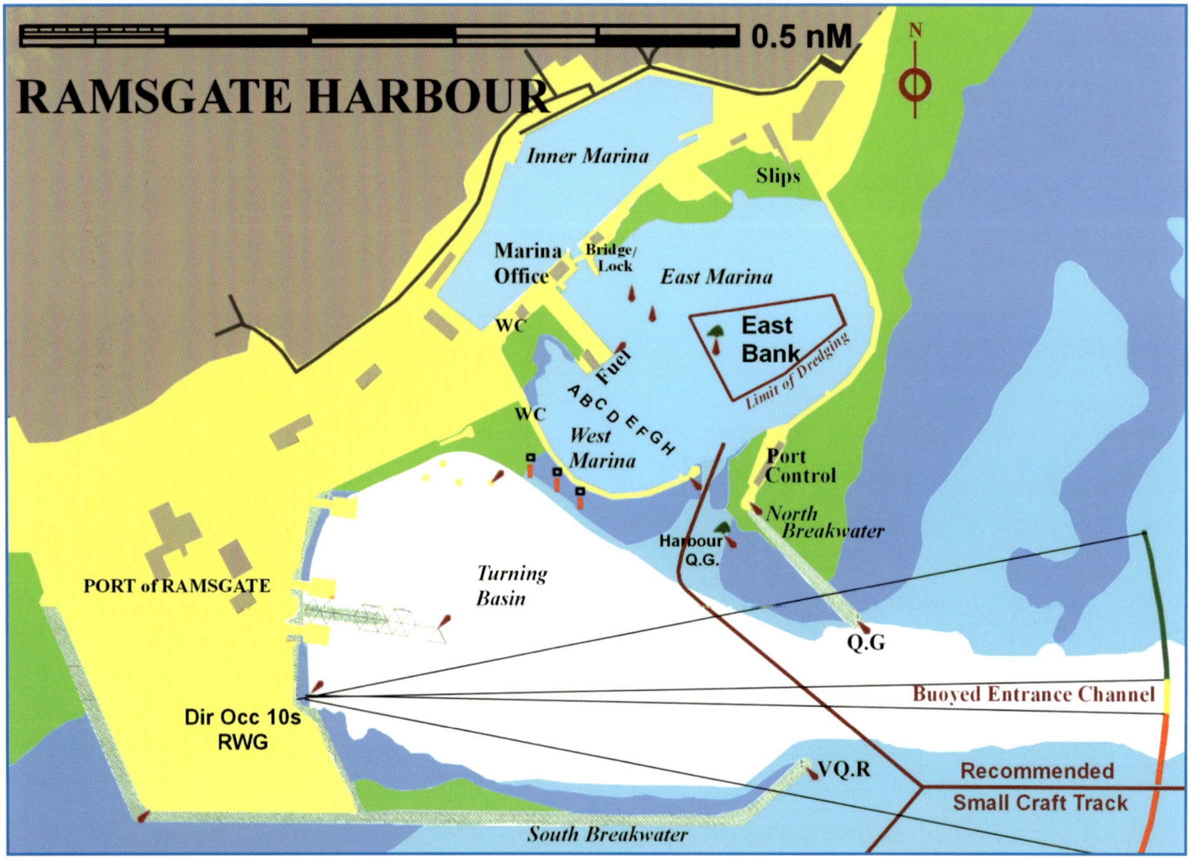

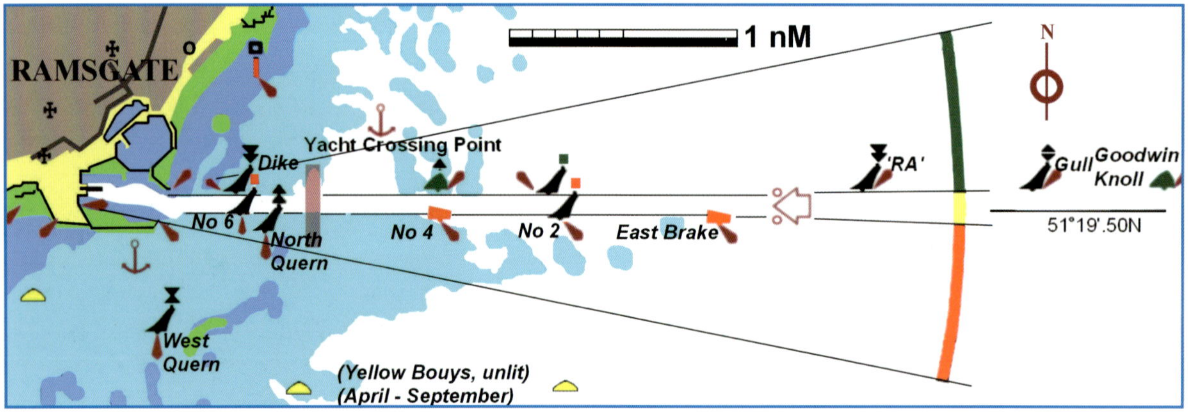

RAMSGATE APPROACH CHANNEL

The Forelands

RAMSGATE

Ramsgate has always been a fishing port, with a breakwater dating from the fourteenth century, but even into the seventeenth century its population only numbered a hundred or so; from then it grew on a combination of local and international trade, and fishing; it expanded further with nineteenth century sea-bathing, from which period is the best of the local architecture. The modern marina is excellent, and the town centre has a reasonable choice of restaurants and leisure facilities.

RAMSGATE – THE MARINAS

THE CLOCK TOWER and MUSEUM

Navigation and Berthing

The Ramsgate approach channel runs due east-west, is well buoyed and a night-time entry is undemanding, but should not be made under sail. The charted channel depth of 7.5m is maintained.

The recommended procedure on gaining the approach channel is to hold a course closely paralleling, but *outside*, the south of the channel to gain the small craft holding area [south]; vessels approaching from the north should cross the channel between buoys ***No 1*** *[QG]* and the south cardinal ***Dike*** *[Q(6)+LFl15s]*; there is also the recommended option of a holding area [north] which avoids the need for crossing the channel pending entry.

Port Control is on the south facing arm of the east pier, and displays the usual IPTS lights *[RRR or GGG]*, and a flashing orange indicates ferry movements during which no other vessels may enter or leave; the clutter of shore lights can make the signals difficult to identify. In any event, permission to enter [or leave] should be obtained. After a departing ferry, the signals may remain RRR until the vessel is long clear, but permission may be given for a yacht to enter in the meantime; some small fishing vessels ignore the signals, but it is better not to follow their example.

RAMSGATE HARBOUR AT LWN+1

RAMSGATE – THE ENTRANCE TO THE OUTER HARBOUR

Entry is between the two breakwaters *[VQR]* and *[QG]*, into the ferries' turning basin; it is appropriate here to request berthing directions, and sails should be furled. Within the basin, which is well sheltered except from the south, the course should about parallel the north breakwater, leaving well to stbd. the shallows marked by ***Harbour*** *[QG]*; a new port hand buoy has also been placed at the entrance. A turn onto about 020°T leads into the Royal outer harbour; this should be made favouring the west pier, and taking care to avoid the shallows under the east pier. Advice as to depths is available from Ramsgate Port Control (VHF CH.14).

Within the outer harbour, there is the modern West Marina with finger pontoons and ample cleats; better than 2m depth is maintained. If berthing anywhere near the entrance, mooring lines should be doubled to cope with a possible heavy swell, particularly with strong south-westerlies. Pontoon 'H' [nearest the entrance] is generally reserved for long-term berth holders, and the long island pontoon is for vessels over 15m in length. Arrivals out-of-hours may take the nearest available berth, and there is a WC block [no code required] on the pedestrian access ramp.

In the unlikely event of the West Marina being full, directions will be given to the old East Marina with similar facilities, although

RAMSGATE – THE ENTRANCE TO THE OUTER HARBOUR

this is usually retained for residents; there is a maintained depth of 2m. The locked Inner Harbour is also occupied predominantly by residents, and is slightly cheaper for a long stay; for locking times [approx HW +/-2hrs] the Marina office should be contacted on Channel 14, and the signals above the lock gates observed; any available outer berth may be used whilst waiting.

Manoeuvring within the harbour requires awareness of the drying East Bank lying between the East Marina and the East Pier, buoyed only at its western edge *[FlG]*, but there is a maintained channel around the perimeter subject to a drying area beneath the East Pier. The fuel barge and pump-out facility are near the lock entrance; arrangements are made through the marina office, from whom a useful range of services is available.

RAMSGATE EAST MARINA

RAMSGATE WEST MARINA

RAMSGATE — MARITIME INFORMATION

CHARTS	Admiralty SC5605.9; Imray 2100.5
TIDAL DIFFERENCE	Dover +0030
WEATHER FORECASTS	Posted at Marina Office
NAVIGATION AUTHORITY	Port of Ramsgate [Thanet District Council] [572100]
SPEED LIMIT	5kts, once inside the breakwaters
HARBOUR MASTER	Ramsgate Port Control VHF Ch 14 [572112]
YACHT CLUB	Royal Temple YC, Sion Hill [571766]
MARINA	West, East and Inner VHF Ch 80 [572100]
	Water, elec, fuel pontoon [P&D], WCs/showers
	40t crane, 5t slip, storage; pump-out
	Some repair facilities
ENGINEERS	
Mechanical	Highway Marine Service Centre [Sandwich] [*01304* 614814]
Electronic	Positive Marine Electronics [*07770* 382920]
CHANDLER	Bosun's Locker, Military Road [Calor & Gaz]
SAILS and RIGGING	Northrop Sails [851665]

STD CODE 01843 ***unless shown otherwise***

RAMSGATE — TOWN INFORMATION

TRANSPORT	
Rail	Ramsgate [1M]
Buses	National Express
Taxis	Central Cars [601601]
	Dee-Luxe [589589]
	Star [581581]
HOSPITAL [A&E]	Q E the Q M, Margate [225544]
Doctor	The Grange Medical Centre, West Cliff Rd [595051]
Dentist [NHS]	S M Ali, 131 High St [592421]
	J Hamill, 73 Hereson Rd [581666]
POLICE	Non emergency [101]
INFORMATION CENTRE	26 York St [restricted hrs] [231055]
	http://www.aboutbritain.co/towns/ramsgate.asp
LIBRARY [INTERNET]	Cannon Rd [593532]
MARITIME MUSEUM	The Clock House, Royal Harbour
POST OFFICES	Margate Rd and Newington Rd
SHOPS, PHARMACY, BANKS	Main shopping in High St., King St. and Queen St
SUPERMARKETS	Waitrose, Queen St; also Aldi, Morrisons and Tesco
YACHT CLUB	The Royal Temple YC, Sion Hill [571766] [bar, terrace, accomm]
PUBLIC	Numerous of similar ambience
RESTAURANTS	There are few for gourmets, but there is a reasonable choice on Sion Hill
ENTERTAINMENT AND CINEMA	Granville Theatre and Cinema, Victoria Parade [591750]
	Grosvenor Casino, Westwood Cross
	Sports and Leisure Centre, High St [585111]
TOWN EVENTS	Ramsgate Regatta week [July/August]
STREET MARKETS	[Fri & Sat]

STD CODE 01843 ***unless shown otherwise***

BROADSTAIRS AT LWN+1

BROADSTAIRS PIER

The Forelands

BROADSTAIRS

Broadstairs was the ship-building centre for the early cluster of Margate villages. The town has grown as a delightfully traditional family resort, with its sandy beach within a stone-walled harbour.

Navigation

The approach is from due east, over the Broadstairs Knolls with patchy shoaling until about two cables off, and midway between the pair of markers *[R]* defining the limits of rock outcrops; the harbour dries inside a line running due south of the pier. With the pier abeam, the aim should be for its point *[2FlR vert]* for the best water in avoiding the crescent-shaped shoal within the bay. On approach,

BROADSTAIRS – DICKENS HOUSE

BROADSTAIRS – BLEAK HOUSE

particular care should be taken for swimmers and toy craft.

There is little space for the casual visitor, and the Harbour Master prefers visitors to anchor off; that said, the anchorage is in firm sand off the beach immediately inshore of the pier, and lines fore and aft are needed. The pier itself is an unsuitable berth for small vessels, and the shore facilities are very limited.

CHARLES DICKENS and BROADSTAIRS

The charming resort of Broadstairs has a long connection with Charles Dickens, who visited throughout his life. Charles first came to stay in 1837, when he was only 25 years old, and while lodging in the High Street worked on the last chapters of Pickwick Papers. However as his friend John Foster said, "The residence he desired most there, Fort house, stood prominently at the top of a breezy hill". In later years he did visit the house, now known as Bleak House, and it provides the viewpoint of the 'Our English Water-Place' a short article Dickens wrote on his beloved Broadstairs:

'In the Autumn-time of the year, when the great metropolis is so much hotter, so much noisier, so much more dusty or so much more water-carted, so much more crowded, so much more disturbing and distracting in all respects, than it usually is,a quiet sea-beach becomes indeed a blessed spot. Half awake and half asleep, this idle morning in our sunny window on the edge of a chalk-cliff in the old-fashioned watering-place to which we are a faithful resorter, we feel a lazy inclination to sketch its picture.'

Dickens continued coming to Broadstairs until 1851 and during his stays he wrote part of many of his novels – Nicholas Nickleby, Barnaby Rudge, Dombey & Son and David Copperfield. Broadstairs of today would be very recognisable to him. The cottage where he regularly had tea with his friend Miss Mary Pearson Strong, and whom he was immortalised as Betsey Trotwood in David Copperfield, is still there on the promenade and is now the Dickens House Museum. The museum retains the parlour described by Dickens and has a fine collection of his letters and personal processions.

Courtesy Kate Wilson, Thanet District Council

BROADSTAIRS	MARITIME INFORMATION
CHARTS	Admiralty SC 5605.9; Imray 2100.5
TIDAL DIFFERENCE	DOVER +0025
NAVIGATION AUTHORITY	Thanet District Council [572100]
HARBOUR MASTER	[861879]
BERTHING	Anchorage [Apply HM]
YACHT CLUB	Broadstairs SC [primarily dinghies] [861373]
FUEL	P&D from garages
MAINTENANCE	As for Ramsgate

STD CODE 01843 *unless shown otherwise*

BROADSTAIRS	TOWN INFORMATION
TRANSPORT	
Rail	[1 ½ m] [N Kent service for London]
Buses	Stagecoach [for Ashford / Canterbury][local for Dover/London]
Taxis	Central Cars [601601] Star [581581]
HOSPITAL	The William Harvey, Ashford [*01233* 633331]
POLICE	High Street [not 24hrs] Non emergency [101]
INFORMATION KIOSK	Promenade [weekends in season]
LIBRARY [Internet access]	The Broadway
MUSEUMS	Crampton Tower Museum, The Broadway The Dickens Museum, The Promenade
SHOPPING	Reasonable general shopping
PUBS and RESTAURANTS	Choice limited but pleasant

STD CODE 01843 *unless shown otherwise*

THE ISLE of THANET

Broadstairs, Margate, Ramsgate

The Isle of Thanet coastline, stretching from Pegwell Bay in the south to Minnis Bay in the North, forms a whopping 20% of the UK–total. It is the longest continuous stretch of coastal chalk in Britain and is completely covered by international and national designations for its marine and bird life - the North East Kent Marine Protected Area. The isle regularly gains more blue flag and seaside awards than any other district in the country.

The 15 sandy beaches and bays carved by the sea from the chalk over millions of years, have been drawing visitors for centuries, with their stunning scenery, soft sand, cliff-top walks, safe swimming and abundant marine and bird-life.

The 1700s' passion for seaside bathing sparked the boom, and the resort towns of Margate, Ramsgate and Broadstairs have a legacy of fine Georgian, Regency and Victorian architecture. Many famous names have been drawn to the Isle; Charles Dickens adored 'delightful' 'fresh' Broadstairs, JMW Turner was inspired by the Margate sunsets and Augustus Pugin built his ideal home in Ramsgate. Tracey Emin declared to Margate 'I will always love you'. Explore these connections at Dickens House Museum, Turner Contemporary art gallery and The Grange. The different histories of the towns, Ramsgate, Broadstairs and Margate, have shaped their character.

Ramsgate with its bustling Royal Harbour and own Meridian Line, five minutes and 41 seconds ahead of GMT, is bursting with continental charm with pavement café and restaurants framing the waterfront. The town has several walking routes that take in the spirit and culture of the town - Maritime Museum, Ramsgate Tunnels and the Georgian Italianate greenhouse. Nearby are the Spitfire and Hurricane Memorial Museum and RAF Manston History Museum.

Broadstairs has retained a gentile old-world seaside charm with its fisherman cottages, retro ice-cream parlour and promenades. Relaxed and unspoilt it is a perfect place to chill out with its wealth of independent shops and inviting cafes, restaurants and bars. The town caresses Viking Bay, but boasts a further six sand-filled beaches and bays, including Joss Bay – a surfer's paradise and Botany Bay, where you can saunter amid towering chalk stacks.

Margate -the original seaside resort, where the traditional delights of beautiful sand, floss and fish and chips jostle for attention with contemporary art galleries, artist studios, chic stores and restaurants. The town's rich history is everywhere - the Harbour Arm, the Shell Grotto and the Tudor House, with further entertainment to be found at The Winter Gardens, The Theatre Royal dating from 1787, and the Tom Thumb Theatre.

http://www.visitthanet.gov.uk

http://www.visitkent.uk

Picture – Turnstones

Article, courtesy Kate Wilson – Thanet DC

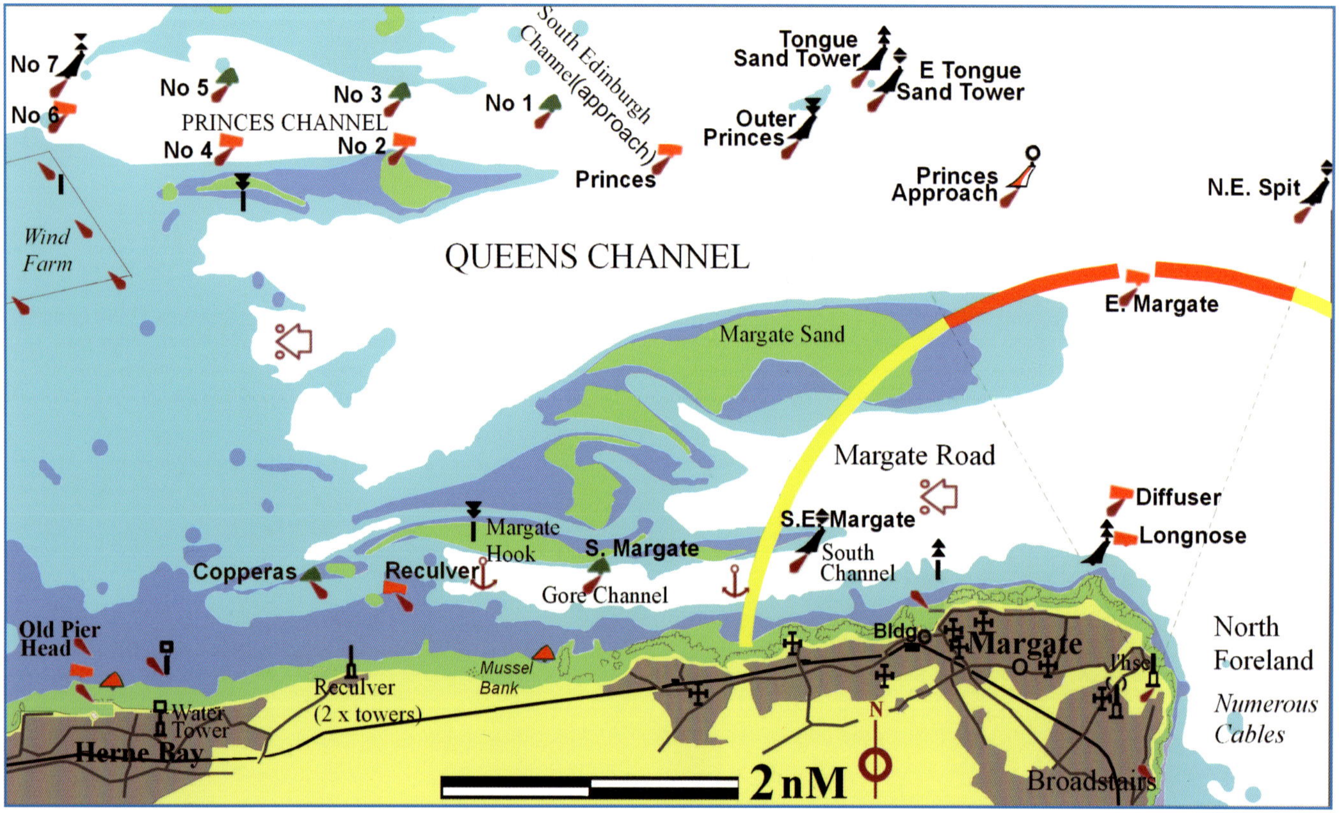

NORTH OVERVIEW – EAST

The North

OVERVIEW

The North Kent Coast is well exposed from the west, and through the north to the east. There are no all-tide harbours of refuge between Ramsgate and the moorings off Queenborough in the west Swale; beaching is usually possible on hard sand at Margate harbour – although tidal and very exposed to the west; Whitstable and Herne Bay harbours are small and tidal; a good anchorage may be found in the east Swale, which provides some protection; indeed, the only shelter from the south west, whilst on passage, is to be found off the Isle of Sheppey where there are also limited [but recognised] landing places. The charts merit careful study with respect to shoaling and commercial traffic channels.

NORTH OVERVIEW MARITIME INFORMATION

CHARTS Admiralty 5500, SC5606; Imray 2100.1,2,3,4

TIDAL DIFFERENCES [approx] on Dover
Margate +0045; Herne Bay +0110
Whitstable +0140; Sheerness +0130
Tilbury +0240

COASTGUARD
Thames [Thames Coastguard Ch 67,16] [01255 675518]

HARBOUR MASTERS
Margate [Foreshore Manager] [01843 577529]
Herne Bay [Foreshore Manager] [01227 266719]
Whitstable [Whitstable Harbour Radio CH 09, 16]
[01227 274086] [Restricted hours]

Weather

This north-facing coastline is subject to marked seasonal differences, and is much affected by continental conditions. The land mass reduces the impact of prevailing south-westerlies, but these still augment offshore breezes whilst reducing those onshore. The effect of colder northerly airstreams is to cause a high incidence of fog when meeting the warmer Atlantic air; this possibility must be considered when passage planning, even inshore.

The exposure to the north can produce severe conditions. A combination of wind over tide, and shallow waters, frequently will produce short and uncomfortably steep seas which make for slow passage making. Conditions can vary rapidly, and substantially, over a small area. It is sensible to telephone ahead, to check local conditions.

Continuous chart updating is vital in these waters, with particular reference to the commercial channels and waters in their immediate vicinity.

NORTH FORELAND and MARGATE HARBOUR

Tides

The Standard Port is Sheerness; from the eastern end of the Swale and eastwards however, local knowledge usually bases tidal predictions on Dover. The tidal flow generally follows the coastline, making to the west, and extending similarly into the Thames Estuary; the rate seldom exceeds 1.5kts, although it will reach 4kts in either direction at Dover HWS -1. Along the north coast, there is slack water between Dover HW -2 & -1.

The Wilsons' 'Pilot's Guide to the English Channel' [1968] states:

At the North Foreland it is high water +0030 Dover. About 3 miles south-eastward from the North Foreland the northgoing stream begins -0120 Dover, spring rate 2.5 knots; the southgoing stream begins +0440 Dover, spring rate 2.2 knots. These times become later further seawards.

In Margate Road the westgoing stream begins -0450 Dover; the eastgoing stream begins +0045 Dover; spring rate in both directions 3 to 4 knots.

….. it will be seen that if a yacht is in Margate Road with a southwesterly wind, it should not attempt to beat around the Foreland until half-ebb to ensure taking advantage of the tide ….

The Thames Estuary is renowned for its sand banks which shift with heavy weather, and both charted depths and buoyage are open to revision; a depth sounder is more reliable than historic soundings. The tides generally follow the channels but, particularly nearing high water, the tidal streams may run across the banks.

The westward passage on a rising tide, and when the flats are made at around lunch-time on a sunny day, provides the opportunity of a luxurious swim in shallow waters warmed by the sand! Anchoring however, must be well offshore to avoid risk of damage to the shellfish beds.

Navigation

THE RECULVER TOWERS

This section follows on from the North Foreland. Here, the cliffs attain about 25m with shoals off, reducing northwards for a mile or so before giving way to the small Kingsgate bay with its sandy beach; immediately to the north is White Ness, with the shoaling outcrops of the Longnose Ledge extending to a near quarter mile from the shoreline.

An inshore course from the south must be better than 230 °T to clear Foreness Point with its shoals extending a near half-mile, and marked by a north cardinal structure *[unlit]*, about on the 2m depth contour. Care must be taken here to avoid the tidal set – in either direction – onto the rocks. With neither the north cardinal nor the buoy ***Longnose*** *[R]* being lit, there are potential problems in conditions of poor visibility or at night time. If there is any doubt as to position, the lit buoy **Diffuser** *[FlR 5s]* about a half-mile to the north and marking the Margate outfall, should be attained.

The westbound passage commences after clearing Foreness Point, and should be well off the north cardinal structure. The cliffs reduce in height towards Margate with its small harbour, and extensive sandy beaches; there is a conspicuous block of flats immediately above. When making the Overland Passage, it should be noted that the Margate Channel, between ***SE Margate*** *[Q(3)10s]* and ***S Margate*** *[FlG 2.5s]* marking the notorious Margate Hook, is here in occasional use as an anchorage for large vessels.

Passage should not be made too close inshore however. Westward, the cliffs regain their height, before a progressive reduction; there are substantial drying outcrops and numerous shoals, and the successive inshore beacons *[unlit]* are perched inshore of the drying heights.

The Margate Channel leads into the Gore Channel, at the northern end of which depths reduce severely. If making for the heads of the Swale Creeks, and running late, there is a good anchorage in sand and shingle off the south cardinal ***Margate Hook***, where there is also a little shelter; the shingle bank emerges with the falling tide, with the rewarding sight of the boisterous gulls descending for the rich pickings.

At the western end of the Gore Channel, the buoys ***E Last*** and ***Hook Spit*** were relocated and replaced in 2012 by ***Reculver*** *[QR]* and ***Copperas*** *[QG]* to good effect, providing a comfortable passage with a minimum of 2m. Here, the twin towers of Reculver, when in transit, bear due south at about 1nM on a small headland; there are shallow outcrops, and at least a quarter mile off is best maintained.

An alternative, for deeper water, is to pass north of Margate Hook; the channel takes a bit of finding, and there is only a half a cable separating the Hook from the sandbank 'Last', before emerging to the immediate west of ***Copperas***. The course from here is much as from ***Copperas*** and should be on about 285 °T, leaving the south cardinal ***Spaniard*** *[Q(3)10s]* well to the north, passing ***Spile*** *[FlG 2.5s]* just on the stbd hand so as to avoid some of the small shallows; a detailed chart is essential, as are the tidal calculations.

Inshore, to the west of the Copperas Channel, is a beacon *[FlY 5s]* marking the outfall from the small resort of Herne Bay; the shoreline here is again of rocks and, above these, is the Herne Bay water tower [conspicuous]. Herne Bay has a small drying harbour and about a half-mile offshore is the isolated structure of the old pier head *[QR]*; this is in a dangerous condition, covered in guano, and a landing should not be attempted.

If making for Whitstable, the entrance is made due south from ***Whitstable Street*** but this is a drying harbour protected by shoals; anchoring off should be avoided in case of damage to the oyster beds. ***Whitstable Street*** *[FlR 2s]* is temporarily relocated to N51° 23.850, E001° 01.348E. The East Swale from the east [see following section], is easiest made in transit between *Spaniard* and **Whitstable**

The village of Reculver, at the mouth of the old Wantsum channel , boasted a magnificent Abbey; twin towers were erected as a thanksgiving for a survival at sea, and these have a beautifully poignant story. Much was lost to French attacks and coastal erosion, but the towers remain and are maintained by Trinity House as a landmark.

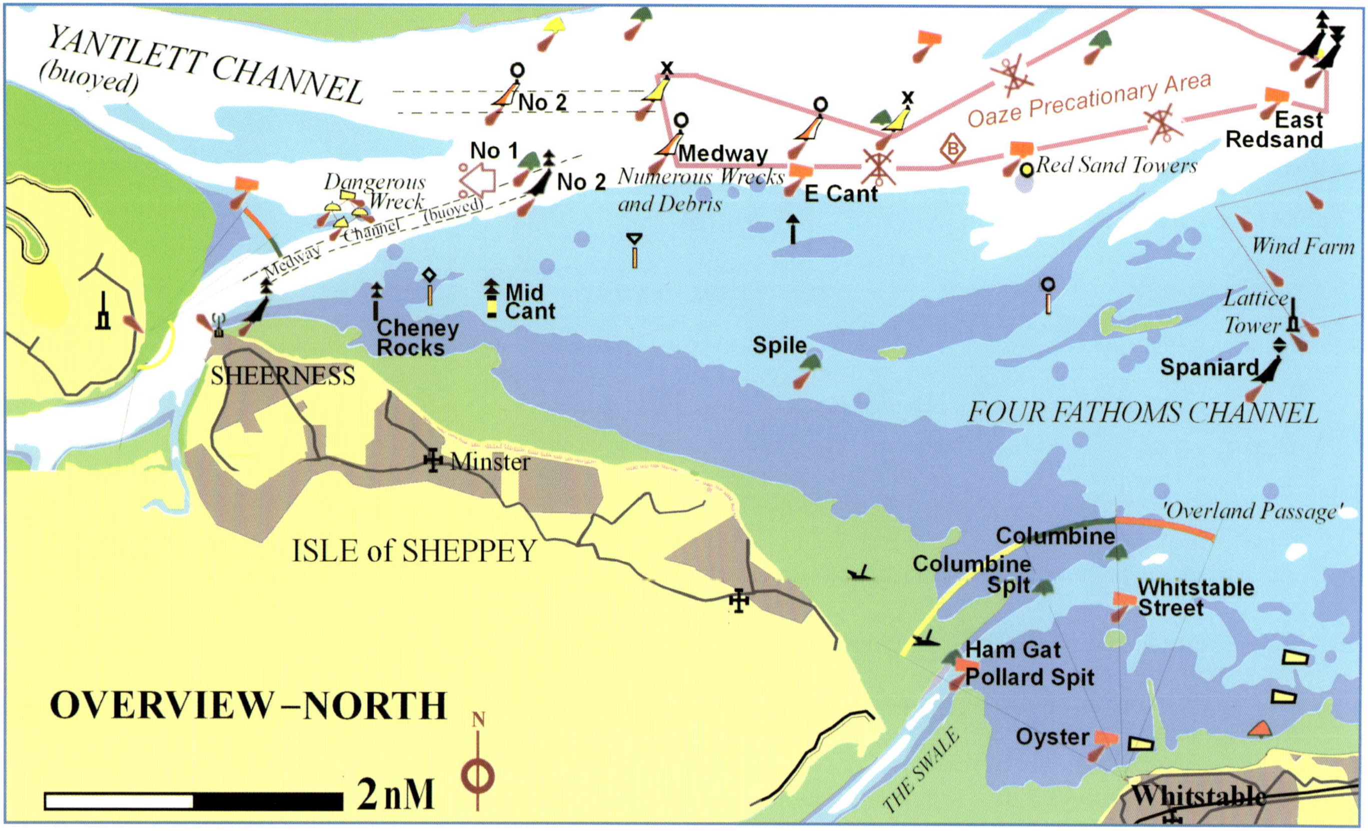

NORTH OVERVIEW – WEST

Street to gain the buoyed channel. If making for the East Swale from the west, the course of 185 °T from *Spile* to the same transit is safe; dependent on the tide, the corner may be cut a little.

The author's preferred northbound passage to cross the Thames estuary, from the East Swale, is to exit on the same transit; from *Spaniard* a course of 345 °T clears the north-western extremity of the wind farm, before turning to skirt the Oaze Precautionary area, crossing the shipping lane, and making for the West Swin, but there are shallows to be considered.

To continue westbound from *Spile*, the course will be about 285 °T fully to clear the shallows of Cheney Spit. The principal landmarks on the Isle of Sheppey comprise the radar station at Warden Point, and the tower of Minster Abbey. There are shallows which extend near 2nM from the island coastline, which are to be treated with caution; the shoreline continues in a generally north westerly direction, comprising a natural sea wall of rocks with a sandy beach

The 'Gat' in the names of Ramsgate, Kingsgate, Margate and Westgate is of Frisian origin, as indeed the 'Gats' of the Thames Estuary. It merely signifies an opening; on land, it is one in the cliffs; at sea, it is one between the sandbanks.

below, but the shallows extend a good mile off westwards from Royal Oak Point, and marked by the north cardinal, ***Mid Cant*** *[Q]*, with little water to the south.

At a mile or so to the west is a safe water mark off Bartons Point, but this is not readily found as it merely comprises a plastic drum; westwards from Bartons point, the shoreline gives way to deep sandy beaches with numerous groynes; dinghy sailing here is active, and supported by the landmark premises of the very professional Sheppey Sailing Club at the commencement of Sheerness town. There is the outcrop of the Cheney Rocks at about a half-mile off, with an unlit north cardinal mark, the topmark and colour of which are obscured with guano. The Sheppey church tower and two chimneys in succession are further landmarks before the radio mast of Sheerness, with the old garrison buildings in front.

There is very little water to the immediate west of ***Mid Cant***, and care must be taken if there is thought to be sufficient water to cross Cheney Spit. The course otherwise should be on about 300°T, for the Medway Approach Channel ***No8*** *[FlR 5s]*, to the southwest of which is the small ship anchorage, and the outside of the channel should be followed, past the north cardinal ***No10*** *[Q]* and ***West Cant*** *[QR]*, before turning for Garrison Point. There is a substantial volume of commercial traffic in the vicinity, and it may well be found appropriate to cross the approach channel at ***West Cant*** to gain the shoreline of Grain Spit, *via* the Little Nore Anchorage, and to enter the Medway on that shore, or similarly for the Thames' Yantlet Channel.

A deep water passage, commencing from Foreness Point, should be made from ***Longnose*** [unlit], on 005°T [185°T] for ***East Margate*** [FlR 2.5s]; when abeam, a course of 270°T [090°T] clears the Margate Sand and leads into the Queens Channel, leaving the south cardinal ***Outer Princes*** *[VQ(6)+LFl 10s]* to the north; this course often provides the opportunity of an extended sail, with a charted depth of better than six metres and few concerns until the Kentish Flats are attained, other than occasional commercial traffic in the Queens Channel. There is little point in adopting the more northerly Princes Channel, other than for interest sake, as this encounters commercial traffic and the close skirting of both the wind farm and the Oaze Precautionary Area – the latter being the turning area for large vessels to and from both the Medway and the Thames, and to and from the English Channel in both directions.

The Queens Channel leads over the Kentish Flats and into the Four Fathoms Channel. The course will, perhaps, have been a little south of west and making for the east cardinal ***Spaniard*** *[Q(3)10s]*, but noting the shoal to the northwest and the numerous wrecks and seabed obstructions. There should be observed the lattice tower *[Mo(U)30s]* at the south west extremity of the Kentish Flats Wind Farm. The array comprises some thirty mast mounted generators with the perimeter marked by yellow buoys *[lit]*; there is no exclusion zone as such, but as unauthorised vessels must maintain a distance of 50m from the masts, the area is best avoided; the seabed service cables run due south to Herne Bay and hence anchoring should not be attempted. Yachtsmen should be aware also of seabed cable laying from the London Array wind farm towards the Swale.

The charted depth over the Flats is uneven and liable to changes, but from the east cardinal ***Spaniard*** *[Q(3)10s]* a course of 270°T [090°T] will find better than 2m charted depth in skirting the shoals of both east Middle Sand and Red Sand; within the Four Fathoms Channel there is a shallow wreck close to the 2m depth contour, and ***Spile*** *[FlG 2.5s]* marks a shallow wreck to the immediate north; the shallows to the northeast of *Spile* should be noted also. The course from ***Spile*** is as described above for the inshore [Overland] passage.

The entrances to the western Swale, the River Medway and the River Thames are described under the respective sections.

A northbound passage from the North Foreland will usually be made on about 020°T [200°T] to clear the Long Sand [off chart, and with revised buoyage] and to remain west of the main shipping routes. An alternative course lies on about 000°T [180°T] for Foulger's Gat *[**Long Sand Outer** (RW, LFl 10s)* and ***Long Sand Inner*** *[Mo(A)15s], both temporarily removed],* leading into Black Deep and thence north-easterly; Black Deep is a major shipping lane to be crossed, but there is the opportunity of tucking into the banks although they are quite steep-to. Yachtsmen should note also that Foulger's Gat is no longer recommended for navigation [2012], although there is no exclusion zone as such.

A more westerly passage for the south Essex coast, dependent on destination, offers numerous choices of threading through the sand banks.

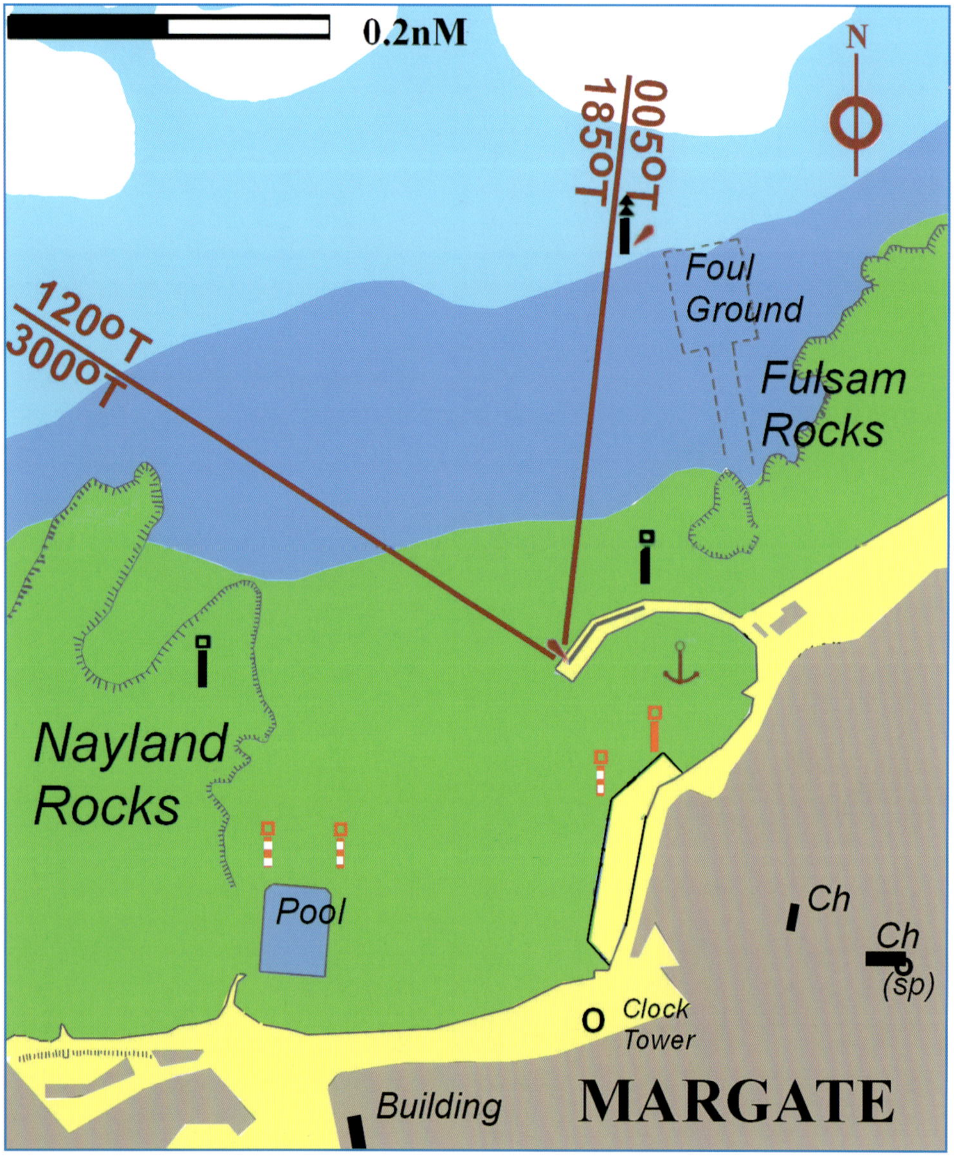

MARGATE HARBOUR

The North

MARGATE

Margate grew from a small fishing village, and subsequently from serving vessels in Margate Road waiting to make North Foreland. The harbour was subject to chronic silting and, when it expanded on the import of timber and coal, a new pier was constructed to the east - but this was demolished in the 1980s; it achieved prominence with its superb sandy beaches and the Victorian advent of sea-bathing; the passenger service from Tilbury was in fishing vessels which could take as many as three days under adverse conditions; there must have been some dreadful experiences! The port was in steady decline in the last century, and in the post-war years its prominence slid to notoriety; eventually, even the Dreamland entertainment centre closed.

There remain some pleasant architecture, adequate general facilities, and a resurgence of interest with the new Turner art gallery at the foot of the pier.

The small drying harbour is severely exposed to the north and west. It has suffered over the centuries from chronic silting, to the extent that there is very little water over its hard sandy bottom, and it is now little used.

MARGATE PIER

THE DROITS HOUSE AND THE TURNER CONTEMPORARY GALLERY

MARGATE HARBOUR AT LWN+1

Navigation

The harbour was constructed in the gap between the Fulsom Rock on the east, and the Nayland Rock on the west. There are less than two cables between the two, and the opening is narrowed by the pier itself.

The approach from the east should be made a half-mile off, not turning in until the north cardinal tide gauge *[Q.3]* is abeam; that from the west will be *via* the Margate South Channel. The safe approach is then from the north and within the lighthouse *[Fl.R.]* sector between 190°T [010 °T] and 125 °T [305 °T], the eastern bearing leaving the tide gauge to port; if closing the lighthouse, it must be remembered that the structure is some 20m within the pierhead.

There were two salt-water pools within the bay. The eastern one, silted, formed part of the harbour wall, and has recent stonework terracing; its projecting western wall remains. The western pool is the more prominent and substantial; both are marked at their outer corners by perches *[R/W & R unlit]*. When the western pool is identified, it is safe to turn towards its eastern side on 180 °T until the pierhead is well abeam.

There is an apology for a channel running east to the pierhead, and occasionally marked by a pair of yellow buoys *[unlit]*, but not worth looking for. The harbour dries to about 2m near the entrance, and up to about 3m within; once inside the harbour, the seabed falls away a little before continuing to rise, and it would be easy to be neaped there. Berthing against the harbour wall finds the best water, but this is prone to sewage contamination and the pier wall is rough with little in the way of ladders or bollards; there are aged iron rings, but only within reach at around HW. Visitors would find it better to sacrifice the best water for an anchorage, where there is good holding in hard sand, and a slipway on the eastern side; there is usually no charge for a short stay, but there are neither facilities nor security.

MARGATE — MARITIME INFORMATION

CHARTS	Admiralty SC 5606.2,4; Imray 2100.5,6
TIDAL DIFFERENCES	Dover +0045; Sheerness -0045
COASTGUARD	Thames Coastguard Ch 67, 16 [*01255* 675518]
NAVIGATION AUTHORITY	Thanet District Council
HARBOUR MASTER	Foreshore Office [577529]
BERTHING	Drying, against pier wall or anchorage
YACHT CLUB	Margate YC 12-14 Fort Hill, Margate CT9 1HD
FUEL	P&D in cans from garage
FACILITIES	Only as for Dover / Ramsgate

STD CODE 01843 *unless shown otherwise*

MARGATE YACHT CLUB (MYC)

The MYC is a very friendly members' club located on North East Kentish coast. The Clubhouse is situated opposite the harbour arm, and has a licensed bar, lounge area and changing facilities; there is also an extensive boat park with a selection of club owned dinghies. Dinghy sailing is the Club's main activity, and the program includes a variety of racing, cruising and RYA training events.

Margate has excellent sailing waters. The drying harbour and the bay provides 1.5 m of water at HW, and provide an excellent area for learners. With access to sheltered launching facilities and sailing, MYC is one of the few clubs on the Kent Coast where sailing can continue through the winter months.

Visiting yachtsmen are welcome.

MARGATE — TOWN INFORMATION

TRANSPORT	
Rail	Margate [1m] [North Kent service for London]
Buses	National Express [local for Dover / London]
Taxis	Central Cars [225487]; United Cars [291133]
HOSPITAL	Queen Elizabeth The Queen Mother Hospital Margate [225544]
POLICE	High Street [not 24hrs] Non emergency [101]
TOURIST INFORMATION	The Pier Droit House, Margate CT9 1JD [577577]
LIBRARY [Internet access]	Cecil Street [*0845* 7200]
MUSEUM	Market Place [231231]
SHOPPING	Reasonable general shopping [High Street]
PUBS	Numerous, but unexciting
RESTAURANTS	Good choice
ENTERTAINMENT	Theatre Royal, Addington Street [292795] Cinema, Westwood Centre [*08712* 240240] Turner Contemporary Gallery, The Pier [233000] [Open Tues – Sun & Bank Hols, 1000-1800hrs]
EVENTS	Heritage Open days [early September]

STD CODE 01843 *unless shown otherwise*

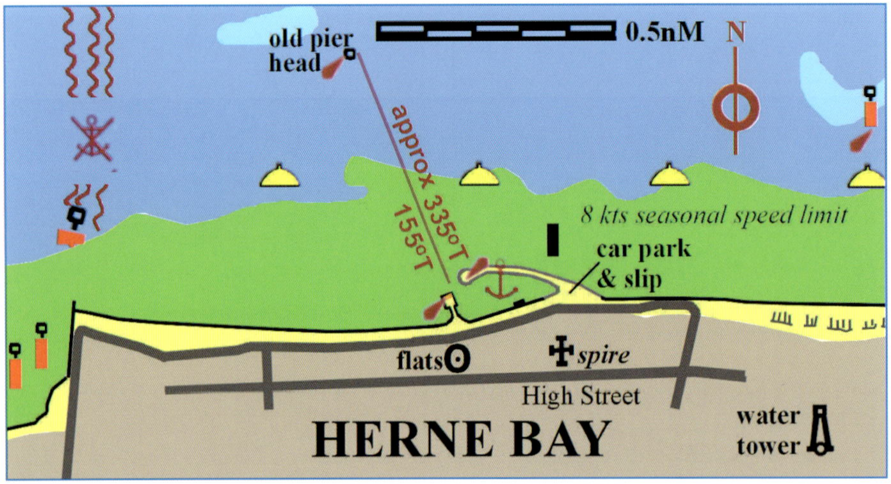

HERNE BAY HARBOUR

HERNE BAY AT LWN+1½

The North

HERNE BAY

Herne Bay remained a small settlement until the advent of Victorian sea-bathing. It retains the ambience of a very pleasant 1960s low-key resort, with adequate facilities. The traditional leisure pier was largely destroyed in the storm of 1986, to the extent that the pierhead remains in offshore isolation whilst the remainder was demolished; the truncated pier has been developed as a leisure centre, displaying the leading lights to the harbour.

HERNE BAY – THE PARADE

HERNE BAY SAILING CLUB

Navigation and Berthing

The small drying harbour is modern, having been created behind a defensive sea wall, with anchorage on the foreshore bank of sand and mud. It dries to about 2m above CD, and rising towards the promenade.

Offshore, at about a half-mile, are the remains of the early pierhead; this is in a dangerous condition, and landing should not be attempted. At about 300m offshore, a series of yellow seasonal buoys are laid to mark the inshore speed limit of 8kts.

The main landmark is the tower block of flats, with the modern leisure centre at the foot of the [part reconstructed] old pier. The charted landmarks of the water tower and the church spire are not conspicuous when closing in. The approach is on about 155°T, to pass between the leisure centre *[vert 2FlG]* and the end of the breakwater *[vert 2FlR]*; the entrance is about 50m in width, and craft need to keep well clear of the base of the breakwater to avoid the protective boulders. The anchorage is on the drying sand and mud bank on the town side, with a slip at the eastern end leading into the car park.

There is some surge through the piles of the pier; the harbour is otherwise quite well sheltered, although seas may break over the breakwater under very adverse conditions. Entry should not be attempted under conditions of heavy weather or poor visibility.

The berths are mostly reserved; visitors are not welcomed, and vessels exceeding 8m overall are even less welcome; a dinghy is needed. There are no specific facilities for the visiting yachtsman.

HERNE BAY		TOWN INFORMATION
TRANSPORT		
	Rail	Herne Bay [1/2 m] [North Kent service for London]
	Buses	Stagecoach [Canterbury/ London]
	Taxis	Abacus [283777] Heron [366666]
HOSPITAL		QEQM, Margate [225544]
POLICE		Gordon Road [not 24hrs]
		Non emergency [101]
INFORMATION CENTRE		William Street [862162]
LIBRARY [Internet access]		124 William Street [374896]
MUSEUM		William Street
SHOPPING		Reasonable general shopping [High Street]
		Saturday Market [Market square]
PUBS		Numerous, but unexciting
RESTAURANTS		Many small cafes and restaurants
ENTERTAINMENT		Kavanagh Cinema William Street [365676]
		The Little Theatre, 44 Bullers Avenue [36004]
		STD CODE 01227 *unless shown otherwise*

HERNE BAY HARBOUR at HW

HERNE BAY HARBOUR at LW

HERNE BAY	MARITIME INFORMATION
CHARTS	Admiralty SC 5606.5; Imray 2100.5,6
TIDAL DIFFERENCE	Dover +0125; Sheerness -0025
COASTGUARD	Thames Coastguard Ch 67, 16 [*01255* 675518]
NAVIGATION AUTHORITY	Canterbury District Council
HARBOUR MASTER	Foreshore Manager [266719, or o/o hrs, 781879]
SPEED LIMIT	8knots, seasonal, inshore
BERTHING	Drying anchorage on mud bank
SAILING CLUB	Herne Bay SC [375650]

STD CODE 01227 *unless shown otherwise*

HERNE BAY – THE OLD PIERHEAD

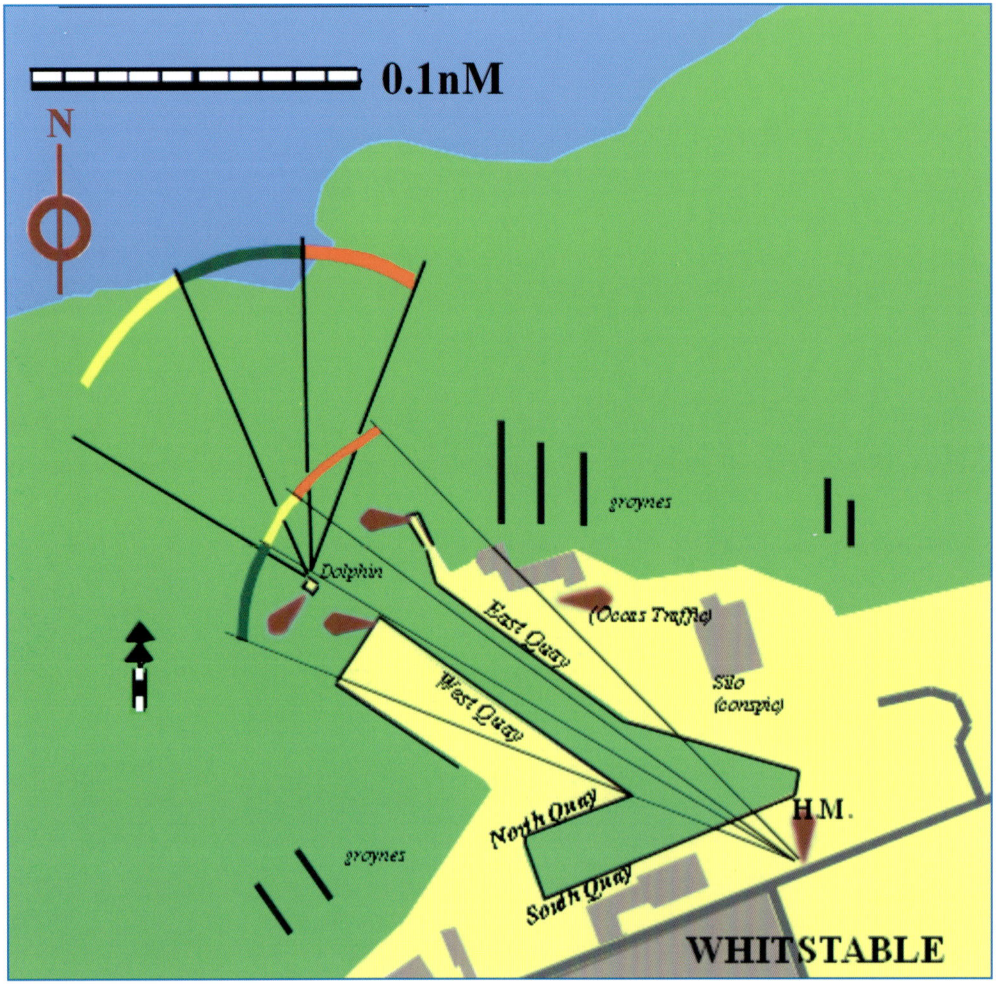

WHITSTABLE HARBOUR

The North

WHITSTABLE

Whitstable grew from a small staging post on the old road from London to Canterbury, but it has had maritime associations from the earliest times. The town has always been associated with its oyster beds of international renown, and it has maintained a strong fishing fleet; Whitstable men long commanded respect for the clearance of wrecks and, indeed, the diving helmet was invented there; it was also the site of the first steam engine – static – for hauling coal up from the harbour.

It remains a commercially busy and picturesque resort; unsurprisingly, there are several good fish restaurants. The crowded and drying harbour however, is not one for the casual yachtsman.

WHITSTABLE BEACH FRONT

WHITSTABLE HARBOUR

Navigation and Berthing

The clearest landmark is the silo on the East Quay, although only for the purpose of initial identification. The approach from the east is from the vicinity of Margate Hook; even keeping at least a mile offshore requires an awareness of the several shallows, and that of the drying tongue of Whitstable Street in particular. The north cardinal *Whitstable Street* has been replaced with a port hand buoy *[FlR 2s]* and, even so, there is a shoal to the south; inshore is *Oyster [Fl(2)R 10s]*. The approach from the north or west will be from between *Columbine Spit [Fl(3)G 10s]* and *Pollard Spit [QR]* marking the entrance to The Swale; *Pollard Spit* however, has temporarily been removed [June 2013].

Inshore of the Swale channel, entry should not be attempted at less than ¾ tide, but HW - 1hr [or HW +1 on departure] is more realistic; there may well be a significant volume of traffic at these times. It will be made on about 335°T from *Columbine Spit* or 297°T from *Pollard Spit*, within the white sector of the Whitstable beacon located on the dolphin at the harbour entrance, and leaving *Oyster* to stbd. The entrance is between the East *[2FlG]* and West Quays *[2(vert)FlR]*, within the white sector of the directional beacon at the head of the harbour. Occasionally, small craft appear from inshore of the dolphin.

There is a speed limit of 8kts between the high water mark and 300m seaward, except in the official corridors marked by two lines of marker buoys.

This working harbour mostly dries, and there is very little available space. Visiting yachtsmen are rare, and the quaysides are not user-friendly except to robust fishing vessels; rafting up to fishing vessels is strongly discouraged, and there are no specific facilities for the visitor. If entry is required, other than in an emergency, the Harbour Master must be consulted in advance.

WHITSTABLE	MARITIME INFORMATION
CHARTS	Admiralty SC 5606.5; Imray 2100.5,6
TIDAL DIFFERENCE	Dover +0135; Sheerness -0005
COASTGUARD	Thames Coastguard Ch 67, 16 [*01255* 675518]
HARBOUR MASTER	Whitstable Harbour Radio Ch 09 12, 16 [274086] [restricted hours]
BERTHING	Drying, against harbour wall
YACHT CLUB	Whitstable YC [375650] Open all year, with good facilities, but primarily for dinghy sailors
ENGINEERS	Request assistance from HM but otherwise only as for Dover / Ramsgate
FUEL	P&D in cans from garage
FACILITIES	Only as for Dover / Ramsgate

STD CODE 01227 *unless shown otherwise*

WHITSTABLE HARBOUR AT LWN+1

WHITSTABLE — TOWN INFORMATION

TRANSPORT

	Rail	Whitstable [3/4 m] [North Kent service for London]
	Buses	National Express [local for Dover / London]
	Taxis	Central Cars [225487]; United Cars [291133]
HOSPITAL		Queen Elizabeth The Queen Mother Hospital, Margate [225544]
POLICE		110 High Street [not 24hrs] Non emergency [101]
LIBRARY [Internet access]		31-33 Oxford Street [*0845* 8247200]
MUSEUMS		5a Oxford Street [276998]
SHOPPING		Reasonable general shopping
PUBS		Limited choice
RESTAURANTS		Several

ENTERTAINMENT

Playtime Theatre, 18 Bennells Avenue [266272]
Playhouse, 104 High Street [272042]
Oyster Festival [late July]
Swale Barge Race [early August]

STD CODE 01227 ***unless shown otherwise***

WHITSTABLE HARBOUR ENTRANCE

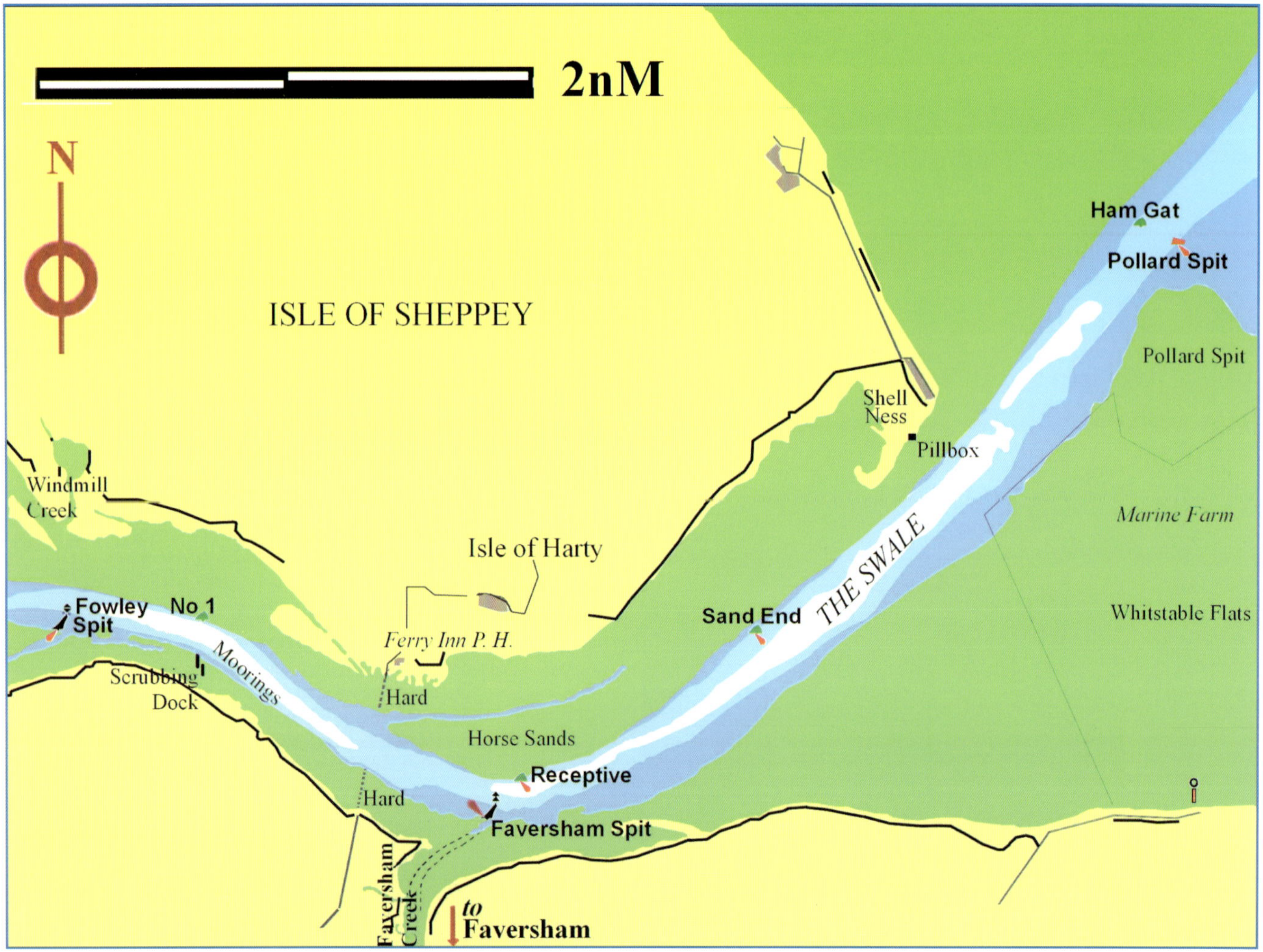

THE SWALE – OVERVIEW EAST
HAM GAT TO FOWLEY SPIT

The Swale

OVERVIEW

The east and west Swale have very different characteristics. The east is pretty, has [for the most part] plenty of sheltered water, and the interesting creeks of Faversham and Conyer; there is very occasional commercial traffic. The western Swale is commercial and rather boring, but has plenty of water and is the obvious route to the Medway and Thames Estuary with a significant level of commercial traffic. All craft using The Swale require a license from Medway Ports.

The only all-tide landing with road access is at Queenborough. Beaching a dinghy at the old Harty Ferry landing south of Faversham is possible.

The Swale has a high point or watershed in the vicinity of Milton Creek, which near dries; it should be noted that the direction of buoyage changes here. By way of general comment on Swale channels, it should be noted also that they vary widely between quite steep-to mud banks or others which are ill-defined.

The waters provide the opportunity for a pleasant sail, but bearing in mind the interruption of Kingsferry Bridge. Night sailing for the length of the Swale is feasible, although there is not much water from Kingsferry until east of Fowley Island, and again little at Milton Creek [The Lilies]; this stretch would be best avoided at less than half tide. A passage through the length of the Swale, in either direction, should commence before half-tide to reach The Lilies at about high water. If at night, and notwithstanding some shoreline illumination, there is a bare sufficiency of lit buoys and the winding nature of the waters anyway disables extended tacks.

THE EASTERN ENTRANCE TO THE SWALE

There is scope for discussion as to whether The Swale is a river, or merely a sunken valley. The former is probably true for the eastern Swale, with its tributaries of Faversham, Conyer and Milton Creeks. The latter is true of the western Swale.

Tides

The Swale tides do not generally follow the 1/12th rule, other than close to the entrances; outside the first and last hours, the rise and fall approximates more closely to a straight line. At the eastern end, the spring ebb at about the first hour can run at 4kts; at the western end the tides call for little comment, although they also can run a little faster than the 2kts suggested by many pilots; at the watershed, the ebb commences at about Milton Creek [The Lilies], but moves eastwards about a mile or so before reversing.

The Standard Port for the whole of the Swale is stated as Sheerness. In the eastern Swale, from below about half tide however, the tidal curve more closely follows that for Dover; indeed, over this stretch, local knowledge bases predictions on Dover but this is irrelevant for the drying creeks.

Navigation

The eastern entrance to the Swale is near featureless, other than for the paired buoys of *Ham Gat [G, unlit]* and *Pollard Spit [QR]*, comprising an obscured channel between expanses of drying mud flats extending from both the mainland and the Isle of Sheppey. It is sensible therefore always to maintain a sense of position, and to identify the two buoys whether aiming for them or not.

Approaching from the east, a shoal-draft craft can make an inshore passage across the Whitstable Flats and Pollard Spit on a rising tide; this gives the obvious advantages of a shorter route, and a decently extended sail. This extensive spit comprises low-lying mud, generally clean notwithstanding some weed, but the contours are uneven and an allowance of at least a metre under the keel is needed; much of this area is occupied by marine farming, and the beds must not be disturbed by either grounding or anchoring.

Approaching from the north-east, there is the possibility of cutting the corner at the Isle of Sheppey, and making for an unmarked swatchway which opens out at Harty on the island shore; again, this needs to be made on a rising tide and only under

HARTY FERRY – THE FERRY INN

good conditions, and taking care to avoid the southern lip of Shell Ness. On either approach, larger craft will need to make for the buoyed channel.

The buoyage is perfectly adequate and, once inside the Swale, the conditions are generally sheltered. The timing of entry is dependent upon the destination; if for Faversham Creek, about two hours before HW at Faversham Spit is best; if for Conyer Creek, where there is a little more water and another hour from Faversham Spit, about two and as half hours is best.

There is good anchoring in soft, but drying, mud to the immediate west of the Whitstable Flats, and again in the swatchway at Harty on the island shore, but taking care to avoid the marine farming; an anchor ball or riding light should be shown. Windmill Creek is not buoyed and is hardly worth exploring; it dries to around 3m, but it can provide a quiet anchorage for small craft; as with most creeks, there is the better water on the outside of the bends, although with turning space only at around high water.

The entrance to Faversham Creek is marked by *Faversham Spit [BW, Fl]*; the spit is growing, and this NCB should be given a much wider berth than charts suggest. Mid-stream, and running up-channel from Faversham Spit to the cardinal *Fowley Spit [BYB, Q(3)10s]* marking the commencement of Fowley Island, is a series of well-spaced mooring buoys which are freely available

Originally, 'Windmill Creek' commenced at the sluice and ran some three miles inland. The present 'Windmill Creek' was originally named 'Crog Dick'; it was the entrance to 'Muscles Creek', and thence to 'Cable Creek' linking with 'New Creek' exiting on the Island shore to the east, and thus defining the 'Isle of Harty'. 'Muscles Creek' is as spelled on early maps; both Cable Creek and New Creek are still traceable although not navigable.

for overnight stays and some have pick-up strops; those, red in colour and at the lower end, are prone to dragging if occupied by craft of more than a couple of tonnes; those, white in colour, and further upstream have been laid by various clubs and yards, and are robust; the showing of riding lights is not here generally observed. These moorings are popular in season, so an early arrival is recommended; doubling up is not unknown, but is resented. Inshore, on the mainland side, are further moorings, but these are private; of passing interest, also on the mainland shore and a little further upstream, are the scrubbing stakes and a hard.

KINGSFERRY BRIDGE – APPROACHING FROM THE EAST

The eastern Swale bifurcates at Fowley Island and the various channels have changed little over the years other than for continued silting. The main channel lies to the north and is fully buoyed. The southern channel provides an approach to Conyer Creek [see below] with minimal buoyage, but extends westwards only as far as the hard of the old Kings Ferry. There is an intermediate creek, the Fowley Channel, in which there is always some water, and which can provide a partial route to the western approach to Conyer Creek for those with familiarity.

The buoyage is easy to follow, through *Nos 6, 8,* and *10 [unlit]*; above Elmley is a pair of posts marking the river bed cables and the channel is at mid point, as between the following North Ferry and South Ferry. but from here the channel becomes shallow and even near HW it's quite possible to drift onto the mud flats!

The tortuous entrance to Milton Creek is marked by the east cardinal ***Lilies*** *[YB, unlit]*, and it is hard now to believe that for centuries this was the maritime highway to Sittingbourne and its major industry of paper making. Pilotage books over the last couple of decades have been increasingly disparaging, and with good cause.

The passage in this direction can be a trifle confusing at first sight, but there's not much of a turn until the Lilies is reached. Here there is the change in direction of the buoyage, and there is a gentle turn to stbd.

The old Kingsferry Bridge, with its impressive brick piers and lifting span, used to be the only hard connection with the mainland, carrying both road and rail traffic. With the new high span motorway bridge alongside, there was hope that bridge lifts for leisure sailing would be less curtailed but this is not the case, and there can be an hour's wait. The rail traffic and, of course emergency services on the road, take priority. There is little point in looking to the rail timetables, because the trains are quite frequent and any late-running throws it all back into the melting pot; bridge lifts will also be held pending commercial traffic serving Ridham Dock.

The approach procedure is to call Kingsferry on Ch10 when about a half-mile off, and to request a lift time; almost invariably, the response will be 'as soon as possible'. If VHF contact cannot be made, it is necessary to call Medway Navigation Services on

Note that some charts refer to 'Fawley Spit', but this is incorrect.

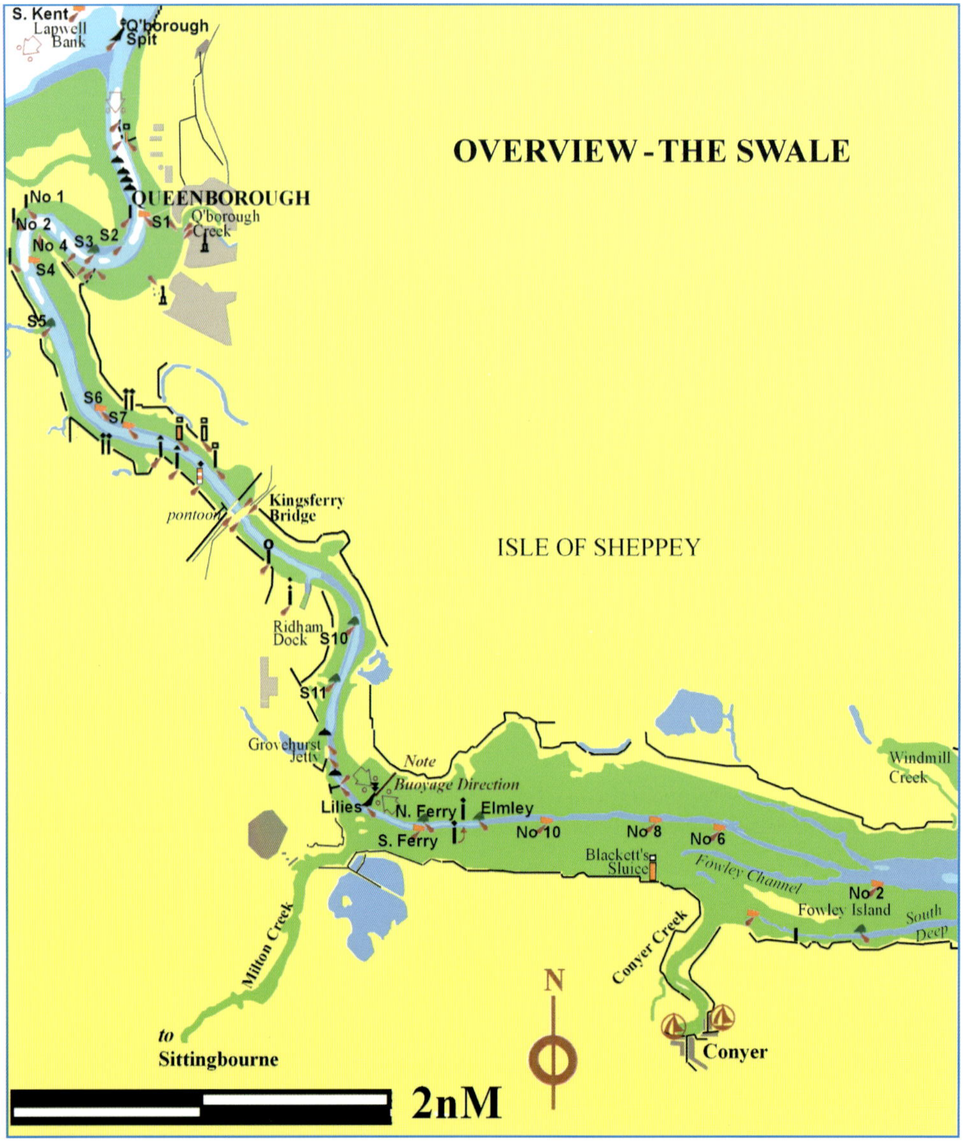

THE SWALE – OVERVIEW WEST: FOWLEY SPIT TO QUEENBOROUGH

Faversham and Milton creeks were of commercial importance well into the 1950s; Conyer Creek was better known for its sailing barges until its residential redevelopment in the 1960s. Conyer Creek Marina is active here.

Ch74 or telephone on 01795 663025; the time-honoured signals of two blasts on the horn, or the hoisting of a bucket, are no longer recognised.

The bridge shows 2xvert. R and G identifying the centre span. The bridge displays Fl R/G when opening, and Fl R/R when closing; it is permissible to pass through when the bridge is not fully opened, but obviously at the skipper's discretion, and not when closing.

On the eastern approach, there are small craft moorings; it is acceptable to berth alongside whilst waiting for the bridge, but care must be taken not to drag the mooring. On the western approach, there is a private pontoon on the mainland shore with about 1.9m of water at HWN; on the island [north] shore, a temporary anchorage is an option but the saving would be negligible. In wet conditions, it is worth practising some 'crabbing' by holding the vessel in the shelter of the motorway bridge. Vessels are expected to be on station at mid-stream before the bridge opening commences, and a listening watch must be maintained on Ch10.

The approach to the Swale from the R. Medway is from between Queenborough Spit and the Port of Sheerness. The course is well marked on the port hand and thence past Queenborough; note that some lights are well above the shoreline. The sea-going tugs berthed off Queenborough are well-mannered, but a lookout should be kept for them nevertheless; when they're called for, they need to respond promptly. To the immediate north of Queenborough, on the island side, there is a pair of dolphins with red superstructures guarding an area of old wharfage and staging which needs to be given a clear berth at all tides. There are possible anchorages in mud, against the western shore.

If approaching Queenborough from the east, the channel is not immediately obvious among the clutter of moored vessels, but is well enough buoyed to avoid grounding on the Queenborough Flats; above half tide, the corner can be cut by passing through the moorings. Indeed, for the western Swale, Queenborough with its all-tide pontoon provides the only realistic landing place with road access; although the facilities are indifferent, it remains popular with yachtsmen.

The passage upstream from Queenborough calls for few comments – this is, after all, the commercial section, although lightly used – and some of the sweeping bends can be cut to save a half-mile or so, but tide dependent. Upstream from Ridham Dock however, and through the Lilies, there is little water and the channel is ill-defined through the mud flats; this is safest at better than half-tide.

Approaching Kingsferry from the west, it should be noted that the buoys *7 & 9 [Q G]* are on inshore structures; the channel buoy *No7A* is more useful, whilst the last port hand buoy *[Fl(2)R 10s]* before the bridge is also on the shoreline. The final approach channel to the bridge is marked by a pair of yellow buoys *[unlit]*.

THE SWALE	**OVERVIEW**
CHARTS	Admiralty 2571, 3683 SC5606.4, 5, 9; SC5606.4; Imray 2100.3,4
TIDAL DIFFERENCES for Faversham	
On Dover	+0125
On Sheerness	+0250
COASTGUARD	THAMES [Thames Coastguard Ch 16, 67] [*01255* 675518]
NAVIGATION AUTHORITY	Medway Ports [969645] Medway Ports Navigation Service [Medway VTS Ch74] [663025]
SPEED LIMIT	8kts [unrestricted for watersports' area W. of Kingsferry]
KINGSFERRY BRIDGE [Lifting]	[Kingferry Bridge Ch 10] [or Medway VTS Ch74 if no response] Clearances at MHWS: Bridge Up – 29m Bridge Down – 3.35m
	STD CODE 01795 ***unless shown otherwise***

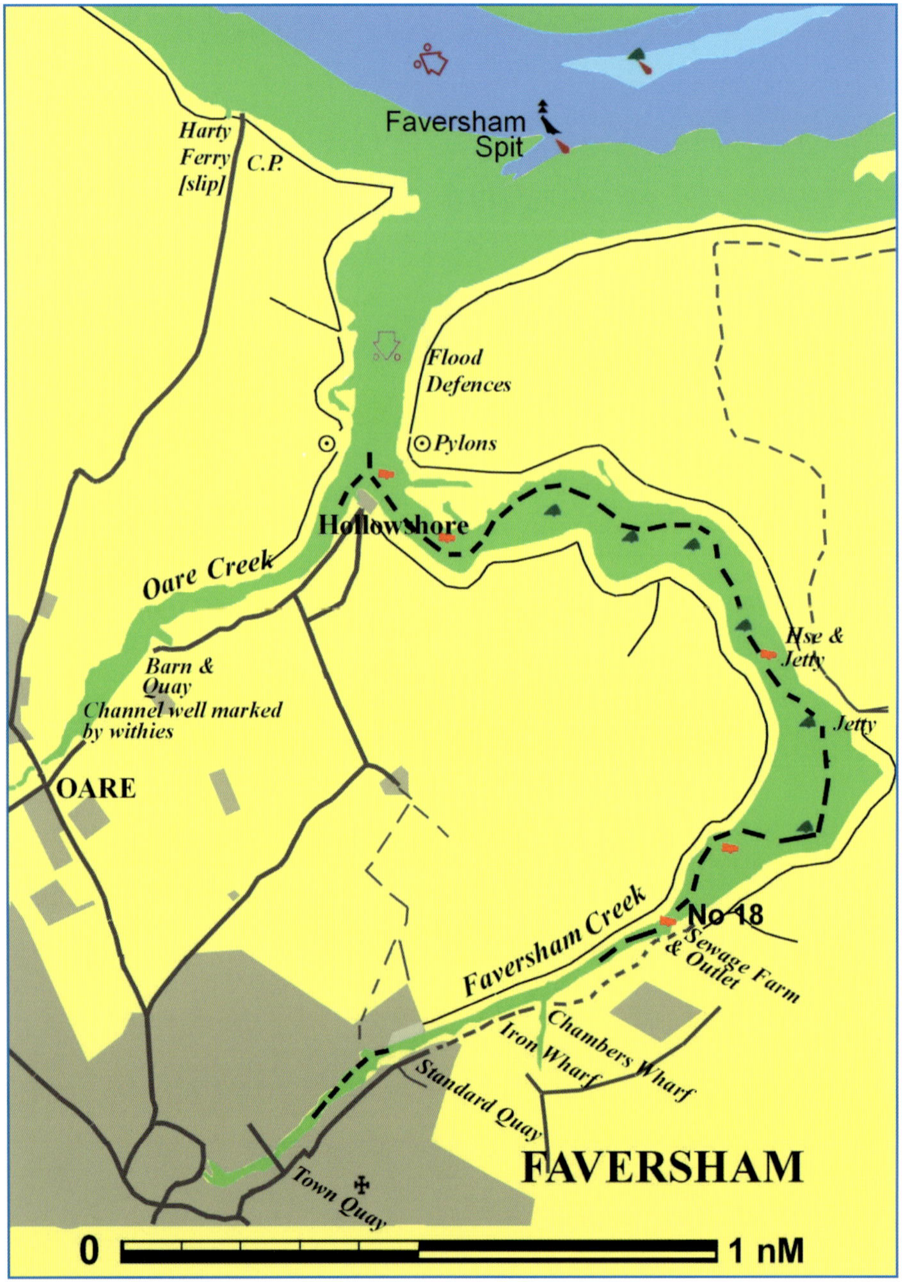

FAVERSHAM and OARE CREEKS

The Swale

FAVERSHAM

Faversham is a delightful and accessible town, with a rich history and some good quality street scenes, having escaped some of the excesses of modern development. The town grew from an agricultural market and distribution centre; notwithstanding its membership of the Cinque Ports, it was unaffected by French raids because it declined to participate in the reciprocal atrocities.

The town offers all daily facilities, including supermarkets and a cinema. There are good bus and rail services.

FAVERSHAM WEST STREET

FAVERSHAM GUILDHALL

Faversham Creek winds some 3nM through a pastoral setting to reach Faversham; on neaps however, there is less than 1.5m of water and there are some shallows to be negotiated. The subsidiary, Oare Creek, has a little more water and is characterised by the numerous mud berths on the port bank. There is an active boatyard at the junction of Faversham and Oare Creeks, and both creeks have boatyards at their head. Neither creek is suitable for a night passage.

The general rule was that, given sufficient water at Faversham Spit there would be sufficient at the head of both creeks, although with some reservation regarding Oare Creek on neaps; with progressive silting, this is not necessarily true, and it should be remembered that a strong southerly wind will reduce the levels. The entry will always be made on a rising tide, and the currents seldom exceed 1.5kts; boat speed should be limited to, say, 3kts to facilitate navigation and to minimise wash damage.

Faversham Creek is usefully marked with unlit buoys; the better water is to be found in the centre of the creek on the straight sections, and by taking the bends wide and otherwise favouring the steeper-to shoreline; the sailing barges should not be followed through shallows, as few draw more than a metre. In the event of grounding, Iron Wharf boatyard may be able to assist during working hours.

The alignment for entering the creek is by holding the vessel in transit between ***Receptive*** *[FlG 10s]* on the island shore and ***Faversham Spit*** *[Fl]* at the creek entrance, and then leaving ***Faversham Spit*** to stbd to gain the centre of the creek; within the creek, the moorings are best left to stbd as there are obstructions on that shoreline. The cluster of buildings ahead, comprising Testers' boatyard and the Hollowshore PH, indicate the junction with Oare Creek running off on the stbd hand; in making Faversham Creek, the buildings are to be left to stbd, but favouring the stbd bank as there are extensive mud flats to port. Oare Creek is described separately.

Towards the head of Faversham Creek, the last buoy is *No18 [R, unlit]*; here, the best water is about midway between the buoy and the end of the fencing on the opposite bank; this is followed by a short and sharp 'S' bend before the channel adopts a gentle bend to port before short lengths of staging and mud berths on the

FAVERSHAM SPIT

port hand, and an old steel barge used as a dry dock; this marks the commencement of Iron Wharf, with the best water at about 8 – 10m off the berths; from here, there are berthing options, but all on drying mud banks. The creek of Chambers' Wharf, occupied by residential berths accessed by a lifting pedestrian bridge, is to be ignored.

At Iron Wharf, short-term visitors are welcome, and there are basic facilities at modest prices, but notice is appreciated and there is little scope for a longer stay; berthing may be alongside one of the regular sailing barges, which obviates the need for shore lines, but ample fendering is always appropriate; the crane wharf must be left clear.

An alongside berth has the advantage of there being more water than against the wall. The predicted depths relate more to Dover than to Sheerness, but the berths against the wall dry to about 3m above datum.

Above Iron Wharf is the slip and shed of Alan Staley, traditional boat builders, and there is no space here for visitors. Upstream, there are the 300m of Standard Quay; this, at five minutes from the

FAVERSHAM – IRON WHARF

town centre, is more picturesque with a cluster of predominantly maritime workshops and the continuing development of facilities; the arrangements are otherwise as for Iron Wharf, and visitors are welcome. Above, there is modern residential development on the port hand, and temporary berthing is possible against the river wall; access however, is not easy. There are private berths against the river wall on the stbd hand.

Further upstream is the area known as The Brents; immediately below the swing bridge [which has not been opened in decades] is the original Town Quay, where there are adequate bollards and a fixed ladder, but with neither facilities nor security; it has the advantages of its being close to the town centre and free of charge for a short stay. Opposite, is a length of staging and security gate, managed by the Council, and available only by arrangement; the nearby Albion PH is popular for both food and ambience.

Oare Creek is gained upstream from the entrance to Faversham Creek. Once past the moorings, there are shore pylons and overhead power lines; before making the turn, it is necessary to continue upstream towards Testers' yard for about 60m to avoid the stbd hand

FAVERSHAM – THE CREEK ENTRANCE at LWN+2

Note the spit at the commencement if Oare Creek

FAVERSHAM — MARITIME INFORMATION

CHARTS Admiralty 2571, SC5606; Imray 2100.4

WEATHER FORECASTS Iron Wharf Boatyard [536296]

NAVIGATION AUTHORITY Medway Ports
Medway Navigation Services [Ch 74,16] [663025]

APPROX TIDAL DIFFERENCES Dover +0hrs55

YARDS and BERTHING

Iron Wharf, Abbey Fields, Faversham
[Iron Wharf Ch8] [537122]
Alongside mud berths to 25m; water, elec, WC/shwr, laundromat, diesel, chandlery tug, crane, dry dock, shore storage, minor repairs

Standard Quay, Faversham [531493]
300m alongside mud berthing; water & elec. WC / Shwr [improvements in hand]; cafe; crane by arrangement; shore storage Dry dock, most yard services available

Town Quay, Faversham [Swale B.C.] [417478]
30m alongside mud berthing, with no facilities Uncontrolled for short stays.

Front Brents, Faversham [FBBAssn] [591140]
30 allocated mud berths to alongside staging; water, elec.

Testers, Hollowshore [532317]
70 mud berths to 12m [few for visitors]; water, elec, WC/shwr, diesel, covered slip to 12t, dry dock to 17m, crane [7t], storage ashore; general repairs/maintenance of wooden boats incl eng.

Youngboats, Oare [536176] [closed Sun, Mon]
100 mud berths, water, elec, WC/shwr, crane [8t] scrubbing grid, chem. toilet and waste oil disposal gen repairs and maintenance arranged deck and cabin cleaning; [chandlery], Calor

FUEL [diesel] Testers [Hollowshore]
Youngboats [Oare]

CALOR [No Gaz] Iron Wharf, Youngboats

CHANDLERS Creek Chandlery, Iron Wharf
[closed Wed, Thurs] [531777]

ENGINEERS - MECH Testers, Youngboats

SAILS Wilkinson Sails [521503]

STD CODE 01795 *unless shown otherwise*

FAVERSHAM — TOWN INFORMATION

TRANSPORT
Rail — Faversham [3/4M]
Buses — Kent C C Traveline [*0870* 608 2608]
Taxis — A1 [538887]; Reeves [536666]
Starlight [24hrs] [591066]

HOSPITAL [A&E] Canterbury [*01227* 766877] [Cottage]
Stone Street [562066]

DOCTOR Faversham Health Centre, Bank St [562011]

DENTIST Hilton, Newton Place [591899]

POLICE Non emergency [101]

INFORMATION CENTRE
Fleur de Lys, 13 Preston St [534542]

MUNICIPAL OFFICES Preston St [594442]

LIBRARY [internet] Alexander Centre, Preston St [594442]

MUSEUM New St [532448]

SHOPPING Good daily shopping, somewhat scattered two supermarkets

PUBLIC HOUSES Numerous, and most serve good food [not Sun pm, Mon]

RESTAURANTS Limited choice, but improving

ENTERTAINMENT Leisure Centre & Theatre

STD CODE 01795 *unless shown otherwise*

FAVERSHAM – THE TOWN QUAY

OARE CREEK – TESTERS' YARD Note the red can marking the foot of the slip

mud flats – there are numerous keel tracks in the mud to prove the point. Having made the turn, there should be observed the two red buoys [unlit] marking the end of Testers' slip, and these are to be left to port; Testers' is a traditional working yard with basic facilities, but visitor berthing is seldom available. This yard is a forty minutes' walk across the fields to Faversham centre, although there is road access of sorts. The adjacent Hollowshore PH is one of the best of traditional houses.

The best water in Oare creek is to be found by tucking quite closely to the mud berths which continue for a mile or so upstream, to an ivy-covered Dutch barn with quay on the port hand; the quayside is security gated. At the quayside, there is something of a pond with a half-metre lip; this makes more difficult any depth comparison with the creek itself, but it is useful if there is insufficient water to make Youngboats' Yard.

OARE CREEK – YOUNGBOATS

Upstream of the barn, the channel is well marked by withies leading to the extensive staging and mud berths of Youngboats; good basic facilities are available there, repairs can be arranged, and visitors are welcome given prior notice; the warning as to tides is repeated, as it is possible to be neaped there. This yard, at a good mile from Faversham centre, is also the base for the Hollowshore Cruising Club.

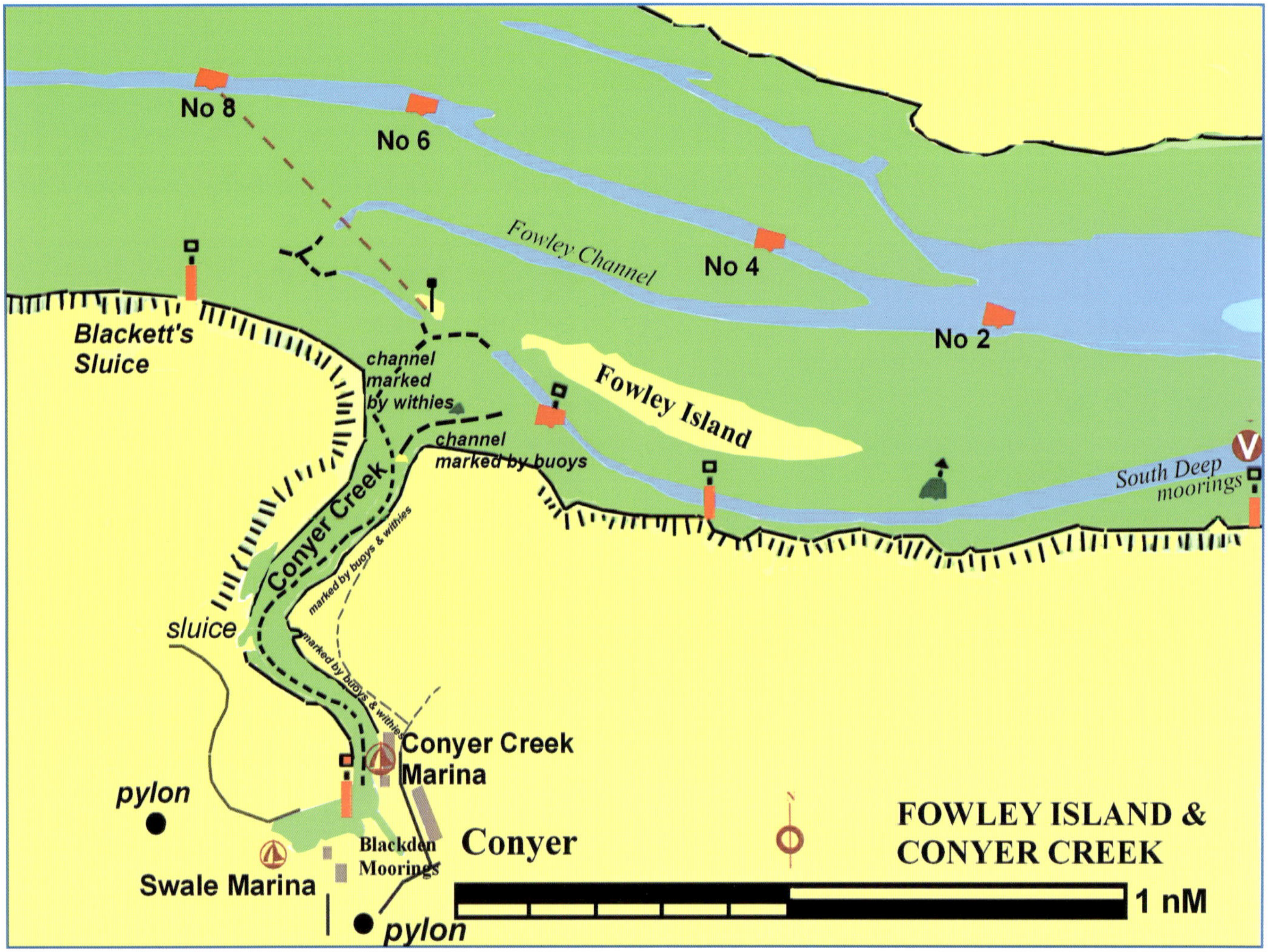

CONYER CREEK

The Swale

CONYER

Conyer was, for centuries, a small centre for the handling of agricultural produce and the building of barges. The Spears' yard, following some waterfront housing redevelopment, is fully operational as the small Conyer Creek Marina. Swale Marina, at the head of the creek, is substantial and well laid out.

The village has expanded somewhat, but without facilities other than for the Ship Inn; this is now in the same hands as Swale Marina, and provides decent food and a deservedly popular bar.

The nearest facilities are at the village of Teynham, at about 1½ miles, but there is a bus service from Conyer through to Sittingbourne. This rural area is popular with ramblers, for its spectacular views across the estuarial marshlands, its wildlife and its industrial heritage.

CONYER CREEK – THE ENTRANCE AT LWN+1½

Navigation and Berthing

There is a choice of approaches from the East Swale to Conyer Creek and the Marina, always to be made on a rising tide; they meet at the inshore side of a mud bank known as 'The Butterfly', and thence into the creek itself.

An approach from the north cardinal *Fowley Spit [Q(3)10s]* leads into South Deep; the best water is found a little S of Fowley *Spit* [say, N51°21.38] and, if in doubt, it is better to favour the mainland shoreline. The course is about 255°T for the green buoy [unlit], which should be given a wide berth; the course is then a little more northerly [say 275°T] which leads into the moorings between the green buoy and the sluice on the mainland foreshore; the moorings, white and four in number, are freely available whilst waiting for the tide; most have floating strops, and there is a minimum depth of 1.6m at LWN. Anchoring on the mainland foreshore, east of the sluice, is not recommended because of obstructions; landing on Fowley Island is prohibited.

The heading from these moorings should be midway between the first red and the distant tip of Fowley Island, before turning into mid-channel of the creek. The creek entrance commences with the first red [unlit and drying] and thereafter the creek is well buoyed to the west cardinal above The Butterfly. This buoy is small and unlit.

An approach from Fowley Bank involves threading through the Fowley Channel from between *Nos2 & 4 [R, unlit]*, but favouring *No2*; the course from *No2* is on about 275°T for 0.75nM. At the western end of Fowley Island there is a small bank with a black topmark *[unlit]* which should be given a clear berth to port before turning onto about 220°T to enter the western channel of the butterfly, which is tortuous but well marked by withies, and thence leading to the west cardinal within the creek.

There is always some water in Fowley Channel, but this disappears quickly when due S of *No6 [R, unlit]*. The turn should not be attempted until the ground beneath the black topmark is well covered.

A third approach is from a little east of *No8 [R, unlit]* in the main channel, and thence turning gently and crossing the mud flats to meet the western end of the Fowley Channel; the continuance is as above. Local knowledge has it that, when the island is covered, 2m of water will be found across the flats to gain a small pond to the west of the island; this is a little optimistic, because there are 3.5m less water across the flats than found immediately adjoining *No8*. This approach is said to find about 0.3m more water than when approaching from South Deep, but there is little in it, and the latter is the easier to follow.

Whichever approach is adopted, the alternative channel becomes apparent on closing in. Any temptation to change channels must be resisted but, in the event of grounding, Swale Marina may be able to assist during office hours.

Upstream from the west cardinal, the best water is in the centre of the creek; this is well marked until the berths are reached on the port hand, where the best water is closer to the pontoons. The creek continues to the Blackden private berths at its head, and the entrance to Swale Marina will be found to stbd.

Swale Marina promises a full range of yard services but, of these, the haul-out was professionally undertaken.

SWALE MARINA

CONYER — MARITIME INFORMATION

CHARTS Admiralty 2571, SC5606; Imray 2100.4

TIDAL DIFFERENCE Dover +0125

WEATHER FORECASTS Available at Swale Marina Office

NAVIGATION AUTHORITY Medway Ports
Medway Navigation Services [Ch 74,16] [663025]

SPEED LIMIT 6kts

BERTHING Conyer Creek Marina [521711]
30 pontoon berths to 12m; water & elec; WCs/Shwrs; full boatyard services. Crane to 9t and shore storage.

Swale Marina [521562]
Tidal alongside and pontoon berths to 12m; some to maintained depth 2m. Crane, slip, storage ashore, yard services offered; WCs/Shwrs, Clubhouse with bar

SUPPORT FACILITIES All otherwise as for Faversham

STD CODE 01795 ***unless shown otherwise***

CONYER — TOWN INFORMATION

TRANSPORT
Rail — Teynham [1½ M]
Buses — Kent C C Traveline [*0870* 608 2608]
Local service to Teynham / Sittingbourne [limited during school hols.]
Taxis - Faversham — A1 [5388867]; Reeves [536666]; Starlight [591066]
- Sittingbourne — A2 Cabs [430400 / 478888]

HEALTH and Information Services As for Faversham

SHOPPING Limited at Teynham

PHs and Restaurants The Ship Inn, Teynham [520881]

STD CODE 01795 ***unless shown otherwise***

The Swale

MILTON CREEK

There is little water to the entrance at The Lilies in the Swale – about 1m at HWN [2010], although there is more in the creek. In 2008, the Barge Museum was destroyed by fire and all the artefacts were lost; subsequently, the sailing club was disbanded, although temporarily resurrected as a private facility with a slipway and pontoon at Milton Wharf near the head of the creek; locals remember swimming there in the 1950s.

There has been wholesale demolition, clearance, and security fencing along the banks pending commercial redevelopment, and even Crown Quay is no more. The creek is no longer buoyed, it is subject to progressive silting, and there are now no recognised landing places; there has been no recent survey, but the depth allegedly dries 1.7m at the new road bridge with its declared air draught of 4.2m. There is no readily available rescue service if a craft should become stranded, and there are no specific facilities for the adventurer.

CROWN QUAY IN 2011

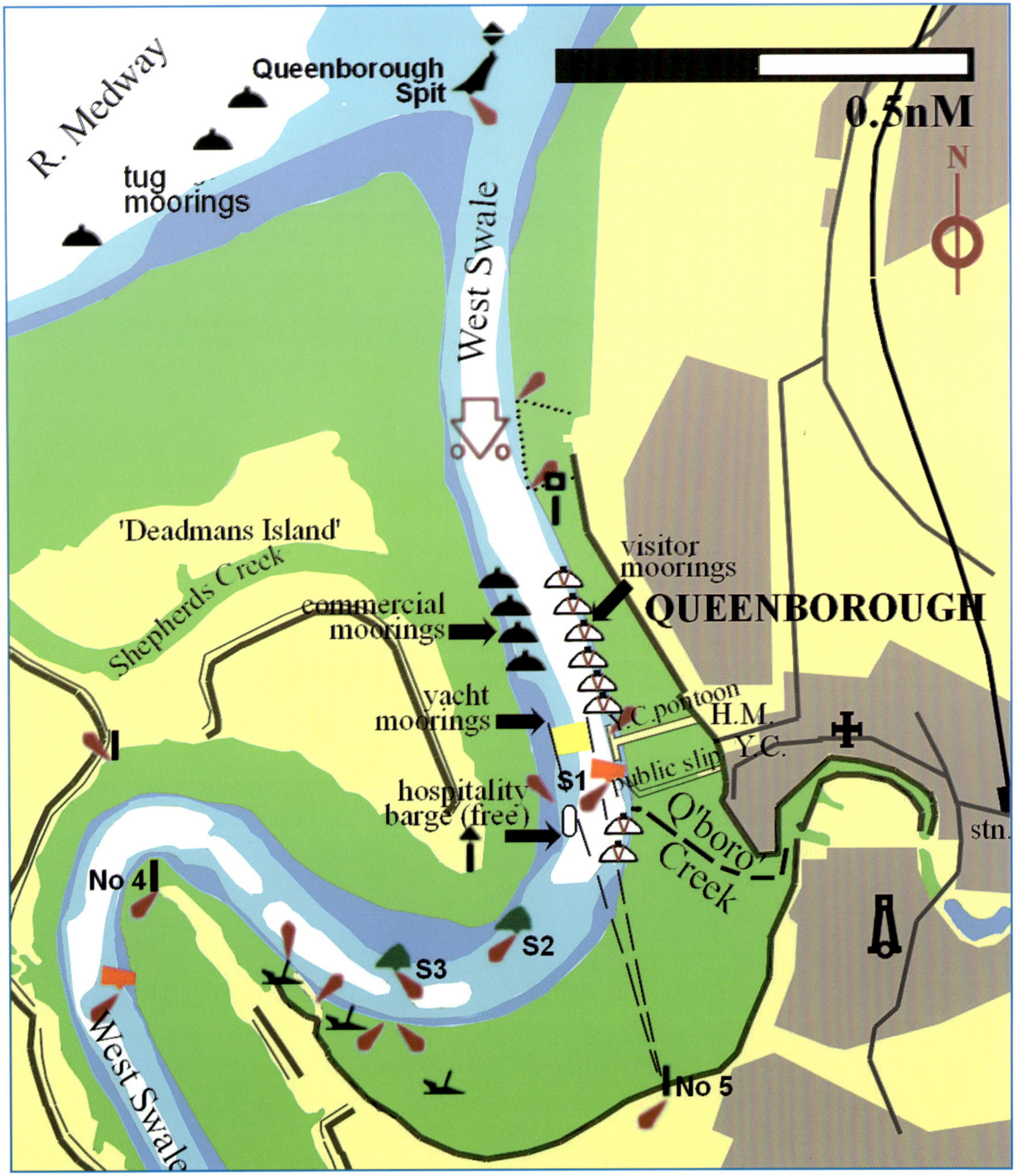

THE WEST SWALE and QUEENBOROUGH

The Swale

QUEENBOROUGH

The settlement grew, from Saxon times, into a medieval trading port which included the handling of large quantities of wool. It was on the safe route from the Thames and Medway, via the Swale and the Wantsum channel, past the port of Sandwich and thence into the English Channel.

Queenborough Castle was built to guard the passage at the time of the wars with France; it fell into disrepair and was demolished in the late 1600s. Shortly afterwards, in common with the Medway, it was heavily attacked by the Dutch. The ensuing improvements to the Medway defenses improved the local economy, but this fell into severe decline with the silting of the Thames' Yantlet creek and Thanet's Wantsum channel; there was resurgence with the increased overseas trading of the 18th century, only to be followed by further decline. With the reduced importance of the Sheerness fort and garrison, the waters became an anchorage for hulks, used variously as isolation hospitals and for prisoners from the Napoleonic wars; the mortality rate was high, and Dead Man's Island was a huge burial ground.

The economy was boosted by the new railway line in 1860, together with a mail and passenger boat service, and with the settlement of new industries. The town today benefits from its proximity to the Port of Sheerness, the tourism of the Isle of Sheppey, and an otherwise mixed economy which includes some small-scale maritime industry.

There are few attractions in the scattered town centre, but it is popular with yachtsmen for its deep water moorings with ready accessibility to the Thames, Medway and the Swale.

QUEENBOROUGH – THE ALL-TIDE LANDING

Navigation and Berthing

The eastern approach from the Swale requires the sharp turn to stbd at Long Point, with better than 3.7m of water at mid-channel between the shoreline beacons *[Q WG* and *Iso R 3s* respectively]. The turn is onto about 040°T [220°T], leaving well clear both the abandoned staging *[2xFlR (vert)]* and jetty *[FlG 2.5s]* on the island shore; at about 0.3nM, the channels turns almost due N into Queenborough Reach at West Point marked by the buoys *S3 [FlG 2.5s]* and *S2 [QG]*, with the Queenborough Flats within the shoreline and the mound of Rushenden Hill behind; there are numerous obstructions on the Flats, in which anchoring is not permitted without the Harbour Master's approval.

The main channel passes closely into the Flats, and a lookout must be maintained for the occasional commercial traffic; here, there are the six buoys reserved to the Swale Fishermen's Association, followed by a pair of visitors' mooring buoys [Y]. Small craft on through passage may save a little distance by turning through the two lines of moorings ahead, which are preceded by a moored concrete barge *[FlG 3s]* best left to port [west] although there is usually sufficient water on the east side.

The entry to Queenborough Reach from the R. Medway entails clearing the N cardinal *Queenborough Spit [Q(3)10s]*, and passing about one cable off the Port of Sheerness on the port hand so as to avoid the shallows on the apex of the shallow bend. At the commencement of the sea wall, the distance off should be maintained to avoid the area of derelict wooden piles [marked and lit *QR* and *FlR 4s*] until the old slipway and a modern industrial unit are abeam; from here, the shoreline recedes to provide a deepening foreshore of mud.

QUEENBOROUGH - THE HOSPITALITY BARGE

Within the Reach, is the all-tide pontoon and hammer-head of the Queenborough YC *[2FlR (vert)]*; overnight berthing is permitted [subject to available space] and dinghy space is to either side. The pontoon is security gated, and tokens for re-entry [£1] are available from the YC, most PHs and some shops.

The pontoon is in course of refurbishment and will be augmented with a further 20m at the downstream end of the hammerhead. This is likely to become available in the autumn of 2014.

To the immediate S is the public causeway, also enabling dinghy access, but it is near-covered at HW and the usual cautions apply. There is a buoy off *S1 [FlR 3s]*, in effect marking both the foot of the causeway and the entrance to Queenborough Creek.

Queenborough Creek, on the island shore, is quite picturesque; it dries to about 3m, but the alongside mud berthing is reserved to residents, for whom there are no dedicated facilities. The entrance to the creek is to the immediate south

LOOKING DOWNSTREAM - DO NOT PASS INSHORE OF THE DOLPHINS! 'Queenborough Spit' is in the background, and the first of the visitor moorings is in the foreground.

of the last workshed on the shoreline. The approach is from a little to the south of the causeway [virtually covered at high water]; the buoyed channel across the Flats is on about 030°T [210°T], leaving the workshed and yard well clear until the creek entrance, identified by the chimney on the stbd hand, is fully open*[R]* and *[2xG]* and can be made on 000°T; there is a tidal barrier, but this is only operated as a flood defence.

Within the Swale at Queenborough, the majority of the visitors' buoys are immediately downstream [N] of the all-tide pontoon; the tide here seldom runs at more than 2 kts. The first is a pair of yellow buoys, to accommodate up to four vessels. To the north are two lines of single visitors' buoys; the inner line *[Nos 1-13]* is uncomfortably close inshore and is not recommended at springs, but may be adjusted consequential upon the pontoon extensions; the outer line [Nos 14-26 and A-D] are in relatively deep water. The buoys are robust, but the pick-up strops are being discontinued. At peak times in season, the HM and the YC between them run a trot boat. Harbour dues are collected on the water, usually with a cheerful 'good morning', at around 0800hrs.

The concrete barge moored off is available for casual landing and, indeed, a friendly barbeque. This facility is under the HM's management.

QUEENBOROUGH CREEK

QUEENBOROUGH LANDINGS

QUEENBOROUGH — MARITIME INFORMATION

CHARTS	Admiralty 2571, SC5606 Imray 2100.4
TIDAL DIFFERENCE	Dover +0100
WEATHER FORECASTS	Available at HM Office
NAVIGATION AUTHORITY	Medway Ports Medway Navigation Services [Ch 74,16] [663025]
SPEED LIMIT	6kts
BERTHING	Apply Harbour Master [662051] Tidal swing moorings [check trot boat availability] Yacht Club pontoon [£1 tokens for security gate] [water at end of public slip]
YACHT CLUB	Queenborough YC [66395] WCs/Shwrs, bar
YARDS	Jim Brett, High Street [668263] *Boat lift and storage, occasional repairs* Brown's Boatyard, South Street [583646] *Crane, slip, limited storage ashore, general maintenance*
SUPPORT FACILITIES	All otherwise as for Faversham, Conyer or Gillingham

STD CODE 01795 *unless shown otherwise*

QUEENBOROUGH — TOWN INFORMATION

TRANSPORT		
	Rail	Queenborough [½M] Shuttle service Sheerness / Sittingbourne, for N. Kent line
	Buses	Kent C C Traveline [*0870* 608 2608] Local services to Sheerness/Sittingbourne
	Taxis – Sheerness	Royal Taxis [61111] Sheppey Taxis [664444]
	– Sittingbourne	A2 Cabs [430400 / 478888]
HOSPITAL [A&E]		Medway Maritime Hospital, Gillingham [*01634* 830000]
DOCTOR		Dr. Ahmed, High Street [583828]
POLICE		Non emergency [101]
LIBRARY [Internet]		[663695]
SHOPPING		Limited, but more at Sheerness
PHs and Restaurants		Several PHs and take-away foods Otherwise Nic's Restaurant, Railway Terrace [661146]

STD CODE 01795 *unless shown otherwise*

SUNSET AT QUEENBOROUGH

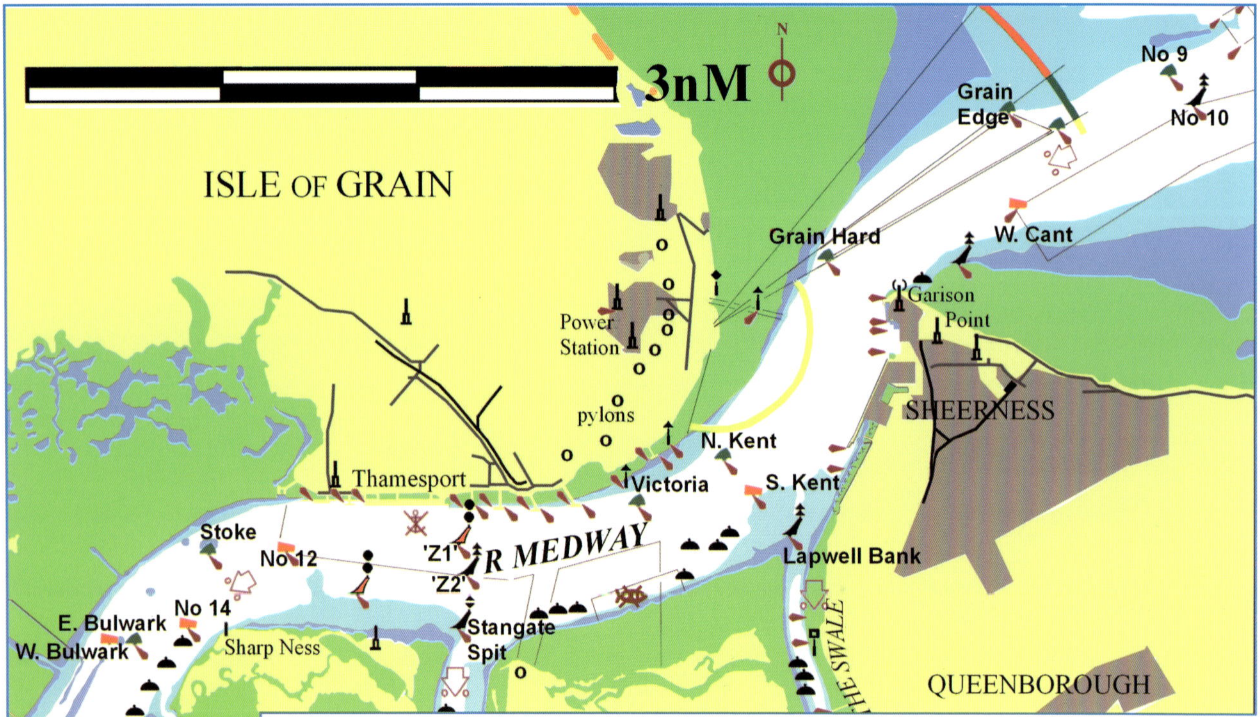

THE R. MEDWAY – SHEERNESS TO HALF ACRE CREEK

THE ENTRANCE TO THE RIVER MEDWAY

The R. Medway

SHEERNESS TO ROCHESTER

The River Medway was, from Roman times, Kent's artery enabling the growth of numerous and extensive industries, which continued into the second half of the twentieth century; it was at Chatham that Henry VIII built the first dockyard dedicated to naval vessels, and this is now a museum not to be missed. The commercial traffic today is concentrated in the lower reaches, serving Thamesport and Sheerness, together with the power stations of Grain and Kingsnorth; on that shore, there are other important wharves too.

The fourteen miles to Rochester offer a deservedly popular cruising ground with numerous creeks to explore, supported by a variety of yacht clubs and the well-equipped marinas at Gillingham and Chatham; there is a good availability of club moorings, and there are innumerable safe anchorages with good holding in mud. The restricted air draft at Rochester Bridge imposes limitations, but the upper reaches are also popular.

The channel is well buoyed up to Rochester, and a night passage is quite feasible given awareness of the commercial traffic. There is a 6kts speed limit above the fort on Hoo Island, and also in the creeks; this is enforced, but it seems to be given a liberal interpretation by commercial traffic. There are areas in which water sports are prohibited.

All craft using the R. Medway require a license from Medway Ports.

Tides

The tidal streams are not strong and rarely exceed 2kts, and those only in the second and third hours of spring ebbs. The main channel is constricted around Chatham Ness and Gashouse Point, with the resulting tendency to push the unwary onto the mud; those under sail should be aware too, of the frequent wind shifts.

The river looks very different between high and low water; initially this can be disorientating as the tidal range at springs is around 5m. The tidal streams within the creeks are much weaker, given the vast areas of mud flats to be covered.

Approaches

The approach from The Swale has been described in the preceding section. The principal requirements are an awareness of Queenborough Spit and commercial traffic.

The approach from the north Kent coast follows the Isle of Sheppey shoreline, not forgetting the shallows [buoyed] extending from Royal Oak Point through to near 0.1nM off Garrison Point *[LFl(2)R]*; Cheyney Spit is a hazard, and it is not until Garrison Point is well abeam that it is safe to turn into the river, taking care to avoid the strong tidal set at the Point. An effort should be made to keep out of the Medway Approach Channel, although there is

SHEERNESS to ROCHESTER MARITIME INFORMATION

CHARTS	Admiralty 1834, SC5606.9, 10, 11,12 Imray Series 2100, Y18, C1
TIDAL DIFFERENCE	Standard Port, Sheerness Rochness, Sheerness +0020
COASTGUARD	Thames Coastguard Ch67, 16 [*01255* 675518]
NAVIGATION AUTHORITY	Medway Ports: Medway VTS [Ch74] Medway Navigation Service [*01795* 663015]
SPEED LIMIT	6kts upstream from ***No25*** [Hoo Island]
LOCAL INTEREST GROUP	Medway & Swale Boating Association *www.msba.org.uk*
MARINAS	Gillingham Marina [280022] Chatham Maritime Marina [899200] Whitton Marine, Hoo [250593]
FUEL	Gillingham and Chatham Marinas

STD CODE 01634 *unless shown otherwise*

little space here; even so, a lookout must be kept for commercial vessels serving the Port of Sheerness. The fort at Garrison Point shows a white flashing light [24hrs] when large vessels are under way.

The approach from the northeast requires planning, in that an early decision needs to be made as to precisely where the shipping lanes are to be crossed. The Oaze Deep and the area immediately to the west should be avoided, as this is something of a Piccadilly Circus for large vessels entering and leaving both the Thames and the Medway; inbound vessels in particular need to be watched very carefully to ascertain their destination. It is better therefore, to gain the Kentish Flats early rather than late, and to make the river as if from the north Kent coast.

The approach from The Thames will follow the Yantlett Flats and Grain Spit, which are deceptively extensive; here a depth sounder is of more use than a GPS. The shoreline of the Isle of Grain should be followed north of the Medway Approach Channel, preferably until the entrance to The Swale is abeam or, say, at *North Kent [Fl QG]*, when the channel may be crossed although this is not obligatory. The approach recommended by the PLA tracks further east, crossing the Medway approach from *Nore Swatch [Fl(4)R15s]* keeping east of *Grain Edge [G, unlit]* for *W.Cant [Y, unlit]* and thence to Garrison Point; this track is near essential at low water. The eastwards extent of Grain Spit should not be underestimated and, between here and Garrison Point, sea conditions can be surprisingly rough.

The passage around Grain Spit – in either direction – merits consideration, because the difference between high and low water is reflected in a distance of near five miles over the ground. It is not possible to make a real recommendation as to passage planning, because of the wide variations in weather and the nature of the vessel; suffice it to say that it can be worthwhile delaying until the spit can be crossed at about one-quarter tide and rising.

The VHF call sign west of the line between *Sea Reach No4* and *Mid Swatch* is 'London VTS' on Ch 68; east of that line the call sign is 'Medway VTS' on Ch 74.

Sheerness to Rochester

The fortification at Garrison Point is matched by the Grain Tower Battery on the Isle of Grain shoreline; there is a low-water causeway between the latter and the mainland, marked by *Grain Hard [G]*; there are numerous cables on the sea bed here, serving the island. Upstream, and into West Shore, the mud flats recede but are interrupted by an outfall channel with black topmark *[Fl(2)G 10s]*.

The island shore, and into The Swale, is occupied by the Port of Sheerness. There are no exclusion zones as such, and the very busy fairway is technically open to leisure traffic. There is no anchoring permitted on the Queenborough flats between The Swale and Stangate Creek, and neither is there off Thamesport; the tall pylon on the tip of the Tailness Marshes is a good landmark, and marks the entry of the submarine cables from the power station. The other conspicuous landmarks are the chimneys of the Grain and

HOO ISLAND AT LWN+1 *(AERIAL OBLIQUE)*

Kingsnorth power stations.

The entrance to Stangate Creek on the port hand, is marked by the east cardinal *Stangate Spit [BYB, VQ(3)5s]*. The best water for the entrance is to be found at about midway between the pylon and the ruined building on the tip of Burntwick Island; this area is described separately.

The shoreline upstream of the Grain power station is occupied by an almost continuous series of commercial wharves and jetties for a couple of miles – these including the Isle of Grain power station, Thamesport, and an LPG terminal; the shoreline here suffers from an industrial ecology, with numerous obstructions; it is well buoyed, and most are lit.

Burntwick island was used extensively as a burial ground, and this building was one of the isolation hospitals dating from the Napoleonic area. Some say that the building has earlier origins, housing the mechanism for a chain boom.

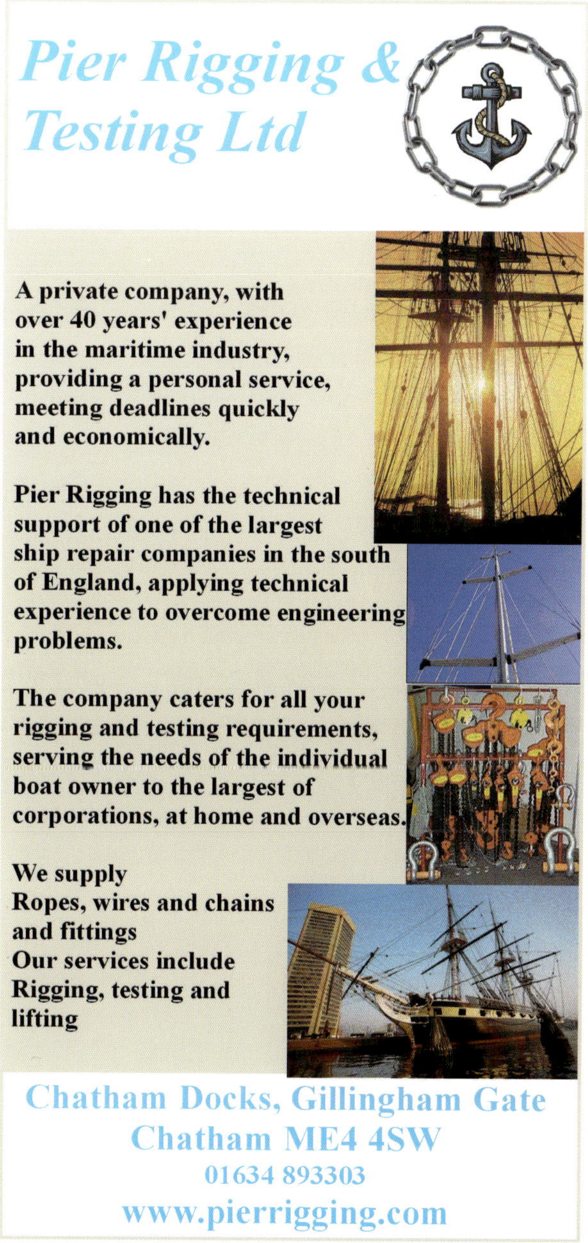

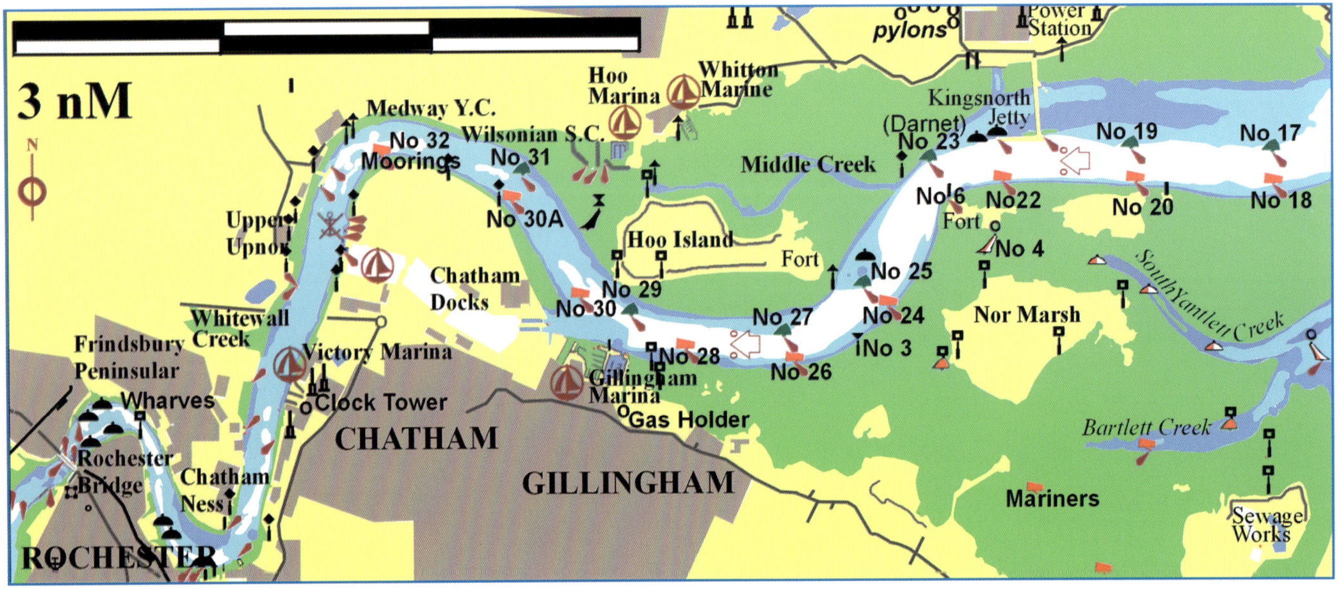

THE R. MEDWAY – HALF ACRE CREEK to ROCHESTER

The Stoke Ooze saltings are on the north bank, as the river turns southwest into Kethole Reach; they are bounded on the southeast by the LPG terminal, and on the south-west by the Bee Ness jetty and dry to around four metres, again with numerous obstructions. Stoke Creek is found on about 320°T from *No14* and heading towards the buoy *G* on the north shore; it does take a bit of finding, and is not worth the effort, unless making for the clutches of private moorings at its head.

The Bees Ness jetty is an abandoned oil terminal for the Kingsnorth power station, and there is a considerable amount of debris on the bottom in the vicinity. East Hoo creek is promising in its course to Damhead Creek to the rear of Kingsnorth; this is no longer used commercially, and the depths are not maintained following the cessation of dredging; the environment however is unattractive and of little interest. Immediately upstream is Oakham Ness, with the Oakham Ness jetty serving Kingsnorth.

On the south bank, there is a line of barge moorings between *No14 [FlR 5s]* and *Bishop No16 [Fl(2)R 10s]*. *Bishop* marks Bishop Spit, and the entrance to Half Acre Creek is between this and the last of the barge moorings; the best water for the creek is found when the Bee Ness jetty terminal bears about 000°T. Stangate and Half Acre Creeks are well worth exploring, and are described separately.

The river turns westerly from *No14*, into Long Reach for a couple of miles, and the south bank here is quite steep-to; on the north bank, is the main Kingsnorth jetty.

The river then turns south-westerly at Darnett Ness, into Pinup Reach; the point is marked by a beacon *No6 [FlQR]*, behind which is a derelict fort; this is matched by a similar fort on the opposite bank, on Hoo Island. There is no landing on either of these

It is necessary to be very clear when calling Gillingham or Chatham Marinas. There is a pronounced signal overlap; some yachtsmen seem to be unsure as to which Marina they are calling or, indeed, in which they are berthed!

THE CHANNEL IS CONSTRICTED AT 'NO 25'

fortified islands, and the 6kts speed limit commences upstream of Hoo Island.

Middle Creek runs behind Hoo Island, giving tidal access to a couple of small marinas and yards, and the Hundred of Hoo Sailing Club; the entrance is a little upstream from *Darnet No23 [G]* and the mark *No1 [BW]*. The creek is otherwise entered from Short Reach, and this area is also described separately as of interest.

On passage upstream, a line from *No1* to *No3 [BW]* on the south bank enables Folly Bank – marked by *Folly Point[G]* and *Folly No25 [Fl(3)G]* - to be cleared.

The mark *No 3 [BW, unlit]*, at the southern end of Pinup Reach, is a little downstream of an un-named and otherwise unmarked creek on the port hand, running parallel upstream with the river, accessing a small boatyard and the Medway Cruising Club. Here, the Cinque Port Marshes dry to around four metres and can be explored fully only on the top of springs.

To the south of Hoo Island, the river turns to a more westerly course into Gillingham Reach, with extensive yacht moorings on both sides of the fairway; the landmark here is the blue-painted gas holder on the southern shore, a little downstream of and behind Gillingham Marina. About 0.3nM downstream of this, is the Medway Cruising Club with its pontoon accessed across the mud flats at better than half-tide; this very active Club is responsible for many of the moorings in the vicinity – they are freely available for an overnight stay, but only some have pick-up strops; those on the inshore line have little water. Immediately upstream is the slip and the SEGAS Sailing Club dock, which does not cater for visitors.

Gillingham Marina adjoins the SEGAS club berthing, and is immediately identifiable by the modern leisure centre on the sea

GILLINGHAM AT LWN+1 1/2

Gillingham Pier is immediately further upstream, with its modern flats' development behind. It comprises a small commercial dock and slip; the pontoon tidal berthing, for twenty or so craft on long-term stay, is security gated. There are no facilities but, given space, the dock is freely available for a quick embarkation.

There are extensive lines of trots maintained by local clubs on the opposite, northern, shoreline. At the western end of Hoo Island a post marks an underwater cable terminal. Upstream, and behind the trots, is a west cardinal [unlit] close to the entrance to the creek serving Hoo Marina, and it is this creek which also passes behind the island, exiting *via* Middle Creek. This area is described separately.

Upstream into Cookham Reach sees further lines of trots of the Wilsonian SC, the Medway CC and the Upnor SC with their

wall, and the blue-painted gas holder in the background; the fuel pontoon adjoins the entrance.

There is a row of waiting buoys outside the marina, freely available, but few have strops. Upstream, is the marina's tidal basin with mud berthing, and with access at about half-tide.

THE RE JETTY

'PORT ASTOR'

Gillingham Pier is owned by a trust for the benefit of the local population, but the river bed is owned by the Council. Berthing against the pier is accordingly free but, if the vessel touches bottom, the Council levies a daily charge.

THE 'THUNDERBIRD' PONTOON with CHATHAM DOCKYARD BEHIND

jetties. The villages of Lower and Upper Upnor are pretty in parts, and there is a couple of good PHs. Immediately above is Upnor Castle, one of the Elizabethan fortifications for the protection of the Medway. Upstream, for a half-mile or so is MoD land and the Royal Marines' jetty [Port Astor]; unauthorised landing is prohibited.

The continuance upstream on the northern shore is increasingly commercial, with modern wharves and transit sheds. Unauthorised anchoring is prohibited from here to Rochester Bridge. On the approach to Chatham Ness, the foreshore deepens, and one should be wary of tucking in too closely. The last wharf of significance is that of the Acorn Shipyard, with premises on the south bank also, and moorings in midstream; this yard is commercial, but will provide a lift-out facility for larger yachts; above are some low-key premises within Bridge Reach, including a USSR submarine, and leisure facilities immediately below the bridge.

The river at Rochester Bridge, and above to Allington Lock, is described separately.

Returning downstream from Rochester Bridge, Gashouse Point on the southern shore is to be left well clear, with the best water to be found at midstream; there may be large vessels manoeuvring here. On the shore, there is near a mile of cleared land awaiting redevelopment; the land is contaminated from its earlier use as gasworks.

Lurking behind some small commercial berths is the Council pier and slip, available for public use at approx. N51° 23'.127; this dries about 1.4m., and is about the only remaining public landing. Below, is Sun Pier, once busy with leisure traffic, but now closed with no plans for re-opening. In the hollow of the bend, between Limehouse and Chatham Reaches, there is a clutch of what were small boatyards which have long since ceased trading to any effect, together with modern development behind.

The next downstream landmark is the tower of St. Mary's

The submarine was sailed from St Petersburg by its Russian crew. It languished optimistically at Folkestone for several years as a tourist attraction, before settling in the Medway as a restoration project with work proceeding 'as and when'.

CHATHAM MARINA and ST. MARY'S ISLAND

Note the Shallows upstream of the Bend

ROCHESTER and SUN PIER

Well into the sixteenth century, naval vessels were commissioned from numerous small shipyards, with the inherent limitation of their being unable to handle vessels of more than three hundred tons or so. This limitation became increasingly unacceptable with increased armaments.

church, marking the commencement of Chatham dockyard. This is followed by the modern offices of Medway District Council, and the long Thunderbird jetty and pontoon; this pontoon supports a mix of long-term yachts and light commercial, including the 'Kingswear Castle' paddle steamer, but an occasional berth may be available although with minimal facilities.

Chatham Marina is identified by the dockyard crane restored and grey-blue painted, perched on the river wall a little downstream of the entrance. The entrance is locked, *[RR, GG]* providing near 24hr access; outside, is the waiting pontoon; this modern marina provides all facilities, including the availability of provisions, although it is a little distant from Chatham centre. The VHF for both Chatham and Gillingham Marinas is Ch 80, and it is necessary to be clear as to which marina is being called.

Returning towards Gillingham Marina, there is an almost continuous double line of trots; most of these have strops, but there is little water at the inner line. The passage otherwise calls for no comment, other than at the point of St. Mary's Island, where *No 32 [R]* should be given a wide berth. Immediately before Gillingham Pier is the eastern entrance to Chatham Docks; the pair of locks receives occasional commercial traffic, and manoeuvring vessels leave little room on the fairway.

Naval shipbuilding at Chatham dates from around 1570 and, by 1588, Chatham had become England's principal fleet base; it was from here that the fleet was prepared to confront the Spanish Armada. The dockyard moved to its present site in 1613.

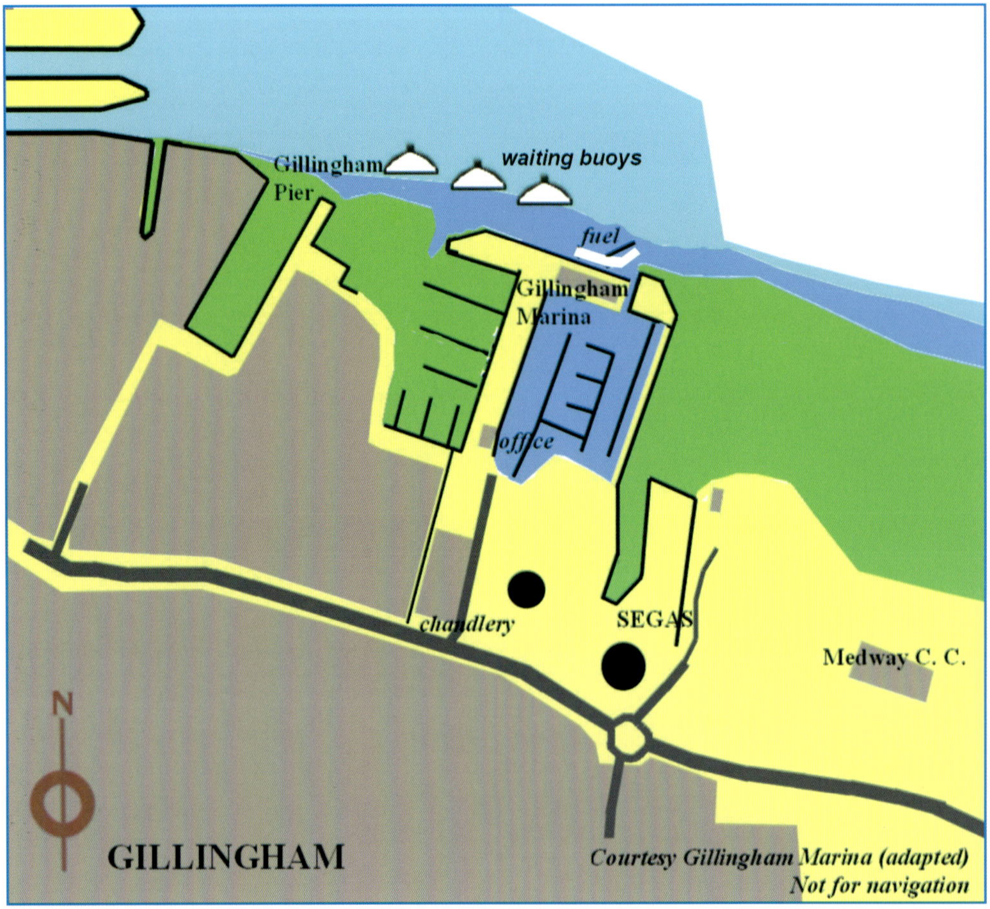

GILLINGHAM MARINA

The R. Medway

GILLINGHAM

The main attraction of Gillingham is its accessibility; when a number of local tradesmen were invited to suggest a defining picture, they were at a loss. That said, the long High Street caters for most needs, but is over a mile uphill from the waterfront; the railway station & taxis are at the eastern end, with the library and a better PH at the western end. Gillingham Marina is a welcome contrast, and there is a convenience store within a couple of hundred metres or so.

Gillingham Marina dates from the early 1970s; it was constructed to a high standard, and hence retains its good quality ambience with the benefit of helpful staff. There is discussion as to the future of the landmark gas holder.

The call sign on VHF Ch 80 is 'Gillingham Marina', whether seeking berthing or merely fuel. The locked basin is accessible for better than ¾ tide, with about 2m maintained depth, the lock is quite small and, even under free-flow conditions, permission to enter must first be obtained ['Gillingham Marina' Ch80]; there are signal lights at the lock entrance [R and G]; the marina has all facilities, including a café/bar open every day during the season, and is well maintained to provide an exceptionally pleasant ambience.

The fuel pontoon, adjoining the lock is inaccessible below ¼ tide and the tidal stream can make berthing a little difficult. The marina's tidal basin with pontoon mud berthing may be accessed from about half-tide; the entrance is close to the downstream wall, and the channel is well illustrated.

Within the marina, there is ample space for turning, but the majority of berths are end-on between piles; the pontoons are modern, and alongside berths may be available at a modest extra charge.

GILLINGHAM FRONT

GILLINGHAM MARINA

GILLINGHAM MARINA MARITIME INFORMATION

173 Pier Road, Gillingham ME7 4LP [280022]
www.gillingham-marina.co.uk
Deep water waiting buoys off

LOCKED BASIN
Access HW +/- 0430; maintained depth 2m
Pontoon berths, mostly end-on, water and elec.
20t & 60t hoists, full workshop with most trades
Shore storage
WC / Shwrs, laundromat, cafe, parking, brokerage

TIDAL BASIN
Access HW +/- 0300; pontoon berthing [mostly end-on]

CHANDLERY Gillingham Marina
Pirates Cave, Rochester [295233]

ENGINEERS Gillingham Marina
Whitton Marine, Hoo [250593]

SAILS Wilkinson Sails, Faversham [*01795* 521503]

RIGGING Pier Rigging, Chatham [893303]

STD CODE 01634 *unless shown otherwise*

GILLINGHAM TOWN INFORMATION

TRANSPORT
Rail Gillingham [3/4M]
Buses Arriva [283600]
National Express [*08717* 818181]
Taxis CNC [818818]
Star [575656]

POLICE Non emergency [101]

MEDWAY HOSPITAL [A&E] [830000]

Doctor Dr Bhasme, 19 Railway St ME7 1KG [853667]

Dentist The Dental Surgery, 84A High St. ME7 1AY

LEISURE CENTRES Members-only centre on site; bar and restaurant access with daily entrance [chargeable] for marina customers and visitors. Public Leisure centre adjacent.

SHOPPING Adequate general shopping in High Street
Convenience store at 200m

PHS AND RESTAURANTS Limited choice

STD CODE 01634 *unless shown otherwise*

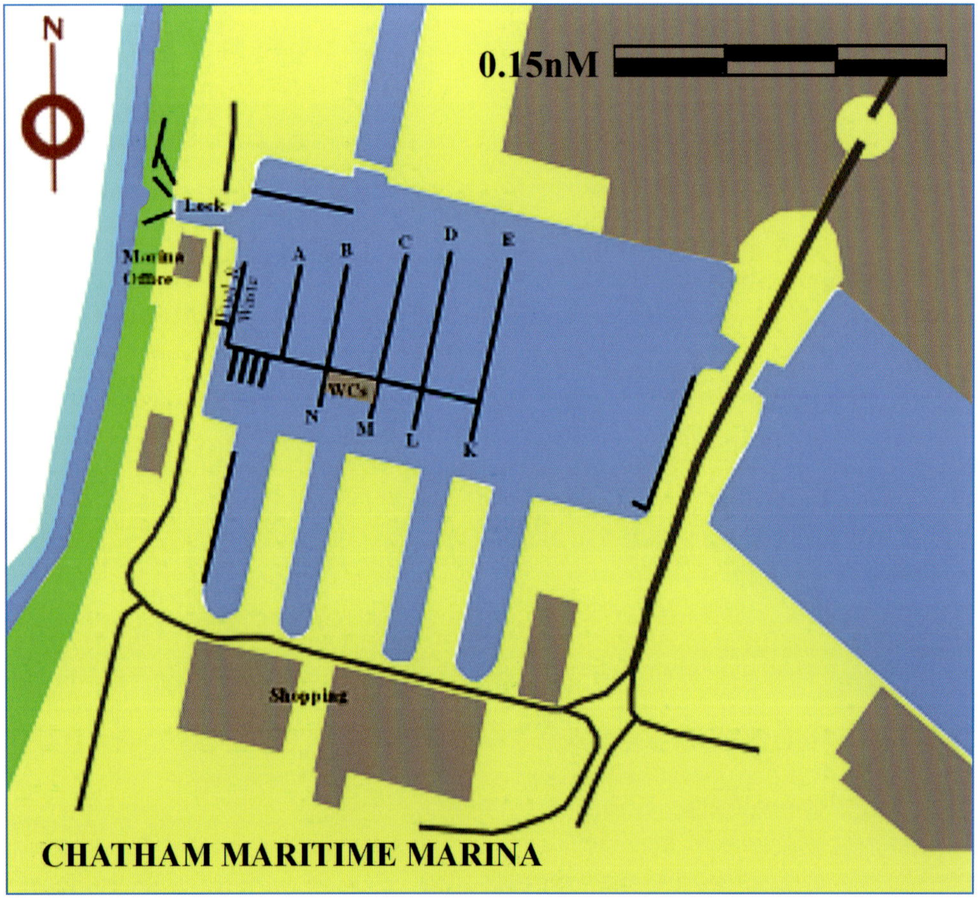

CHATHAM MARINA

The R. Medway

CHATHAM

Chatham Marina is within No 1 Basin of the old naval dockyard. The area has seen major residential development extending the 1½ miles to Chatham centre - from which transport communications are good; in between, the attractions are few - other, of course, than the adjoining Chatham Maritime Museum.

The Marina is upstream of Gashouse Point *No 32 [QR]*, and commences with the grey-painted dockyard crane on the river wall; a little upstream is the visitors' pontoon, adjoining the lock, and the tide runs strongly here. The upstream landmark is the 'Thunderbird' pontoon.

The call sign on VHF Ch 80 is 'Chatham Marina' for berthing or fuel requests; a mobile phone call is acceptable [01634 899200]. The lock is open 24hrs, but the sill is restricted to about 1.5m at MLWS; there are better than 2m depth maintained within. The Marina facilities are good, although very typical of modern developments.

THE ENTRANCE TO CHATHAM MARINA

CHATHAM MARINA

CHATHAM MARINA — MARITIME INFORMATION

Chatham Maritime Marina
Leviathan Way, Chatham Maritime ME4 4LP [899200]
www.chathammaritimemarina.co.uk

LOCKED BASIN
Access 24hr, but sill restricted to 1.5m at LWS
Waiting pontoon [chargeable]
Pontoon berthing [side-on] with water and elec.
WCs/Shwrs, Laundromat, MDL WiFi
20t boat hoist, storage ashore
Maintenance services by arrangement

SAILS Wilkinson Sails Faversham [*01795* 521503]

RIGGING Pier Rigging, Chatham [893303]

STD CODE 01634 ***unless shown otherwise***

CHATHAM — TOWN INFORMATION

TRANSPORT
Rail — Chatham [1 ½ M]
Buses — Arriva [283600]
National Express [*08717* 818181]
Taxis — ABC [840840]
Star Taxis [363636] Vokes Taxis [222222]

POLICE Non emergency [101]

MEDWAY HOSPITAL [A&E] [830000]
Doctor — The Medical Centre, 29 Bryant St. ME4 5QS
Dentist — Gibraltar House, New Road ME5 0TX [862749]

SHOPPING Factory outlets on site
Convenience store at 200m, otherwise at Chatham

PHs and Restaurants Limited choice on site

STD CODE 01634 ***unless shown otherwise***

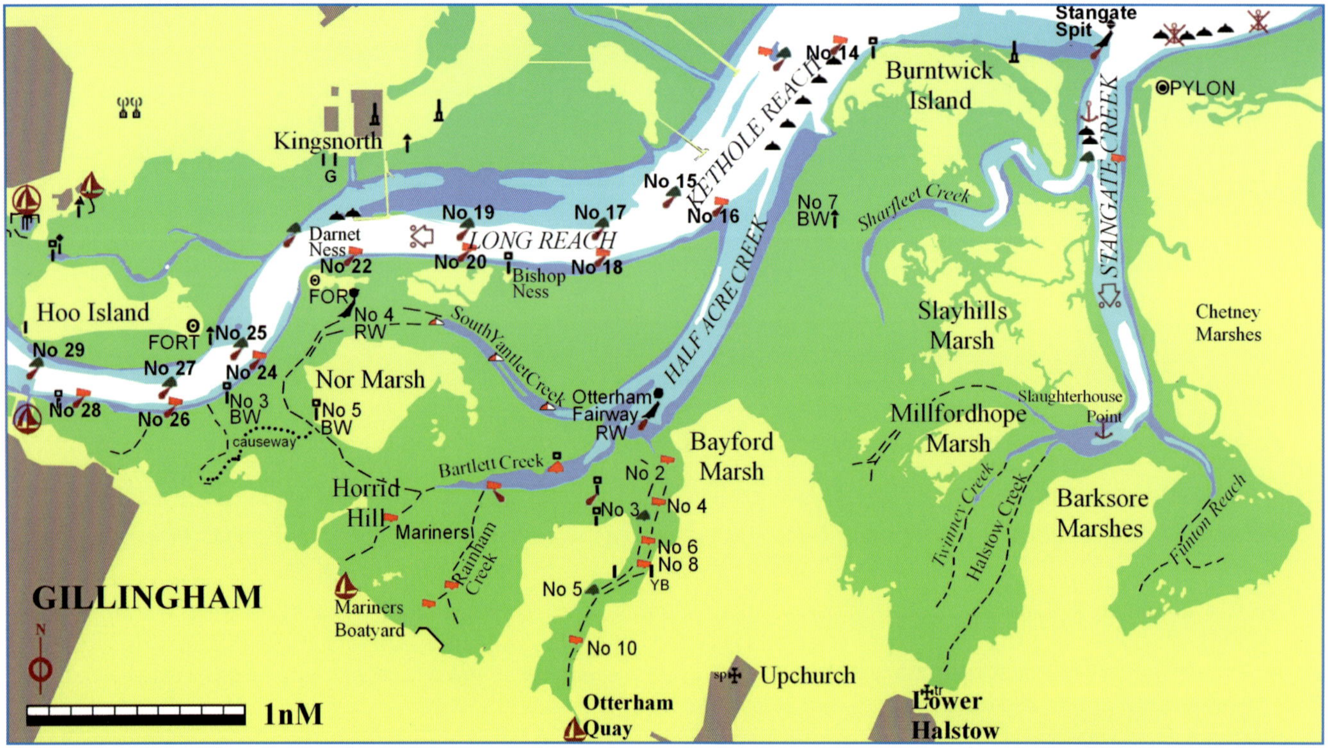

RAINHAM MARSHES

THE ENTRANCE TO STANGATE CREEK

The R. Medway

STANGATE & HALF ACRE CREEKS

Stangate Creek

Stangate Creek, and its neighbouring Half Acre Creek, provide a delightful and popular contrast for those who have enjoyed a boisterous sail in the Thames Estuary. In the creeks, which remain uncrowded, there is the opportunity of practising boat handling and position fixing in well sheltered waters [the power station chimneys and the Swale bridge are almost always in sight]. There is a sufficiency of weed, however, to discourage swimming and landing on the islands is not pernitted.

There is sufficient water for most, in the couple of miles of Stangate creek at all stages of tide. The entry is best made from Saltpan Reach, about due south of the N Cardinal, and east of the East Cardinal, midway between the tall pylon and the derelict building on the tip of Burntwick Island; at about a quarter mile there are the channel buoys *R* and *G [unlit]*, and below these is a couple of barge moorings. The barge moorings are occasionally used by a dredger, and there is a charted anchorage below; caution needs to be exercised however, as there is some abandoned tackle on the creek bed which can readily foul an anchor – an anchor buoy can be helpful here. There is a drying channel dividing the island, but this is not navigable.

The channel divides at the southern tip of the Sharfleet Saltings, with Sharfleet Creek winding in a westerly direction; this creek is not buoyed, but is readily navigable. When the mark *No7 [BW, unlit]* bears about 310°T, a safe course is on about 260°T at half tide to cross the Ham Ooze and gain Half Acre Creek; it is better to err by keeping to the south of this course, rather than letting a southerly breeze take one onto the shallows above. Captain's Creek is a risky alternative crossing.

Below the Queenborough Marshes, Stangate Creek offers the choice of Funton Creek and which is readily navigable for a half mile, after which it peters out in a series of meanders which are not very interesting; in earlier days it served a brickworks.

The basin below Slaughterhouse Point offers a safe anchorage with good holding in mud. Milfordhope Creek looks promising at first sight, but there is little water and the channel to the small boatyard at Shoregate Lane takes some finding.

Twinney and Halstow Creeks however, are more promising and lead to the Lower Halstow moorings and Sailing Club; of the two creeks, Twinney looks to be the better, but becomes all but impassable before the destination is reached. Halstow Creek is very well defined on the river bed – it is a narrow trench – and the entry is at about midway between the Barksore foreland and the small island to the west; there are no navigation marks or really useful transits, but the rather inconspicuous tower of St Mary's church is a useful pointer. Without familiarity, it is a matter of locating the creek by depth sounder, and it is better to approach a little from the west as, at the commencement, there is a shallow patch inshore. There will be found better than 2m at HW +/- 1 on most tides.

The Stayhills and Queenborough Marshes were long used as natural sheep pens – as evidenced by the evocative Slaughterhouse Point.

LOWER HALSTOW AT LWN +2

At Lower Halstow, there is an extensive group of moorings; these are mostly licensed by the Medway Ports, but a few are privately laid. The Lower Halstow SC facilities are limited, but include a jetty, slip, lift-out and shore storage with WCs / Shwrs in progress. There is also a private wharf at the head of the creek, and which is home to a sailing barge; to the north-west of the wharf, there are the remains of an old causeway which can trap the unwary. This is all in a very pleasant environment, and the nearby Three Tuns is worth a visit.

Half Acre Creek

Half Acre Creek used to serve the local waterfront industries and commerce of the Victorian era; apart from it being a useful cruising ground, it is not of special interest other than for its industrial archaeology and some wildfowl. Landing is not permitted on the islands.

The creek has a generous entrance from Kethole Reach, a little above the line of barge moorings and below *No16 [Fl(2)R 10s]*, and with water at all tides. The first mile provides a clear passage down to the safe water mark of *Otterham Fairway [Mo(A)10s]*. The creek there continues in a westerly direction into the South Yantlet channel with a series of three centre channel safe water marks; there is a centre channel shoal between the first and second. At the third, the depth reduces rapidly, drying to about 1m above datum, but there is always water at better than half tide; there are moorings to be avoided. The course continues westerly to the final safe water mark, where the exit into Pinup Reach is best found by aiming for the fort on Hoo Island and holding in transit the distant block of flats; it is better to err on the southerly side of the track.

At *Otterham Fairway* a buoyed channel leads southerly into Otterham Creek. On the stbd hand there is an odorous sewage works, but the wildfowl seem not to object; a pair of markers

THE RAINHAM SALTINGS: To the left, Otterham Fairway is out of sight; the bifurcation of South Yantlet Creek is on the extreme left; the promontory of Horrid Hill is mid-left, with the creek to Mariners Boatyard behind. Sharpe's Bay is to the right of Horrid Hill, and Burntwick Island is on the bottom left; note the very tight channel adjoining Burntwick Island.

indicates a seabed cable. A little further upstream is a defunct boatyard on the port hand; from hereon the depths need to be watched, but it remains navigable at HW +/-1½ for most tides; at the head of the creek is Otterham Quay, with lift-out and boat storage, but with no other facilities.

Bartlett Creek also leads from *Otterham Fairway*; the buoyage is minimal, but adequate, and Rainham Creek leads off. The entrance is marked by a red can *[Fl(2) 5s]*; a back sight onto the safe water mark in South Yantlet Creek is helpful, and must clear the drying Nore Marsh; if there is poor visibility for that back mark, it would be unwise to proceed further, and navigation is anyway on depth sounder notwithstanding the couple of buoys. The creek bifurcates to serve a couple of small and derelict wharves, and the charted building is inconspicuous. The derelict Bloors Wharf is approachable at HW +/- 0100, but is rough and not a recognised landing, notwithstanding road access.

There is a further creeklet at the drying end of Bartlett Creek, leading south-westerly across the Rainham Saltings. An informal red can marker has been laid [***Mariners, unlit***], and the course is then on about 225°T for the continuation; this leads into a pleasant area of small craft moorings, and to a slip with breakwater [port hand side] on N51° 23.12', E000° 35.95' [GPS derived]; there is road access, and it is used by the Mariners Boatyard.

The continuation of Bartlett Creek is past the promontory of Horrid Hill; at the head of the small bay, marked by an abandoned barge, there is a long defunct wharf and a few moorings. It is not worthy of exploration, although of possible interest to industrial archaeologists.

It is possible to continue west, below Nor Marsh, to regain Pinup Reach. This is feasible on the top of most tides, but it is very difficult to find the charted depths [this is shown on the bottom left of the Rainham Saltings panorama]; the creek is not at all well defined on the river bed, but the safest course is to continue north past the western point of Nor Marsh and regain the South Yantlet Creek.

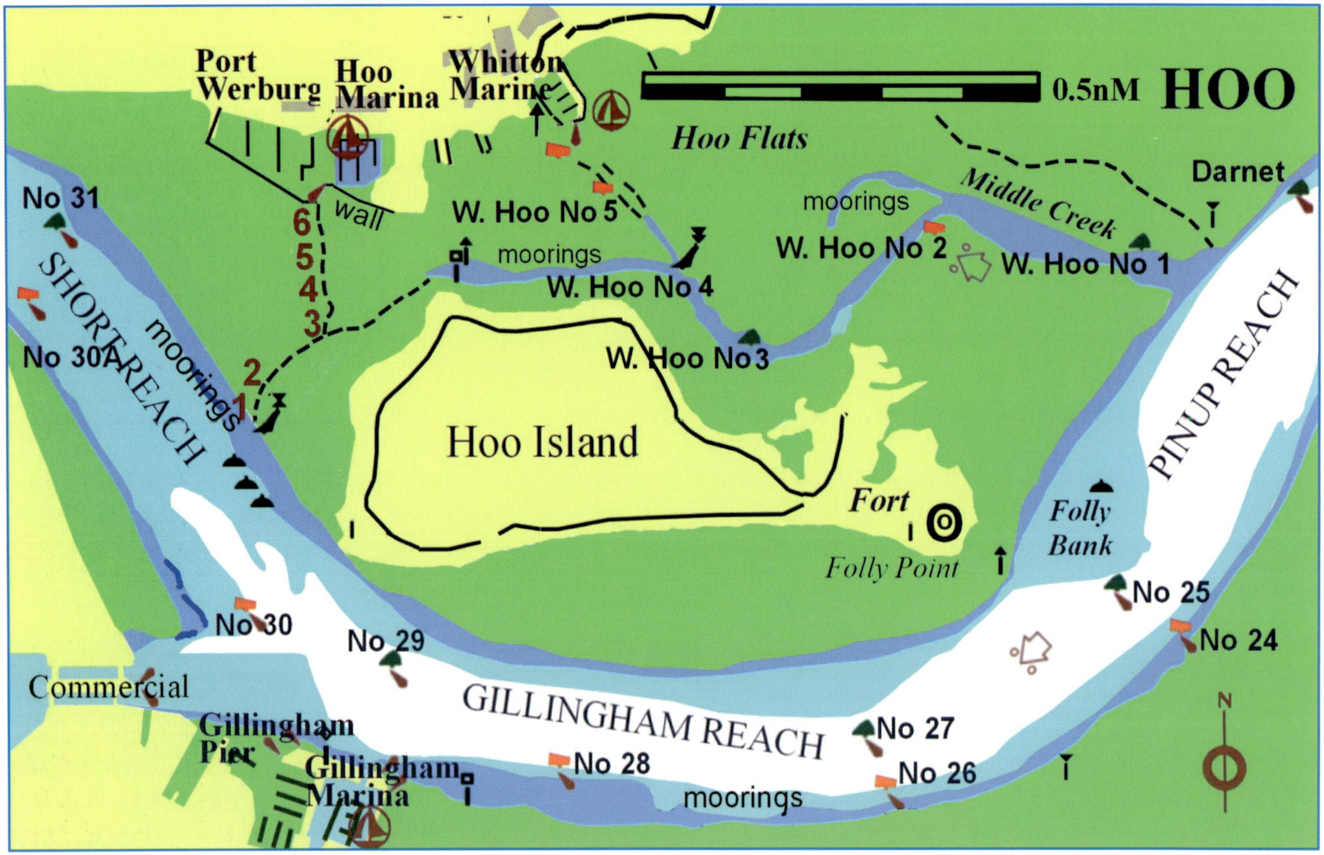

THE HOO FLATS

The R. Medway

THE HOO FLATS

Middle Creek, with its extension behind Hoo Island before returning to Short Reach, provides access to a clutch of yards and a marina on the Hoo peninsular. The main length of the creek is well defined on the sea bed; although there is a noticeable variation in depths, there is usually better than 2m of water at half tide. A combination of depth sounder and good visibility is necessary.

A course of 290°T from the point of Darnett Fort leaves the mark ***No1** [BW, unlit]* to stbd upon gaining the creek and, on the same course, a green buoy will also be left to stbd. At about 0.2nM a further buoy will be left to port, after which the southwesterly direction of the creek will need to found, and this passes close to the tip of the island; the creek then follows the bay at about a cable off, before turning northwest. A pair of stakes will be observed to the west and, when these bear about 270°T, the channel forks.

THE HUNDRED OF HOO SC

THE WEST OF HOO ISLAND AND HOO MARINA

The northerly fork heads towards the small boatyard of Whitton Marine and the Hundred of Hoo SC; there are drying shoals off to stbd, but the channel is not too difficult to find, with about 2m depth at HW +/- 1.

The westerly continuation is towards the pair of stakes marking the gap in the old causeway between the mainland and the island; there are long term moorings here. The depth then reduces rapidly and the channel must be followed with care, but near 2.5m depth is to be found at HW +/- 1.

The southwesterly continuance leads to a channel marked by withies; a stbd turn leads to Port Werburgh, whilst a port hand turn leads back over the flats to Short Reach. The approach from Short Reach is *via* 'the Orinoco Channel', with better than 2m water at the top of tide; the channel is well marked by withies, although subject to minor changes and the withies are prone to damage.

At the marinas' shared entrance, Port Werburgh is to port, and comprises residential berths only. The yacht marina to stbd is modest but well run, with about 2m depth maintained beyond the sill, and the facilities are more than adequate; visitor berths are not currently available. The residential and yacht marinas are now under the same ownership.

THE ORINOCO CHANNEL	WAYPOINTS
1 West Cardinal	N51°24'.22 E00°33.'29 cs 020°T
2 Withy to be left to port	N51°24'.23 E00°33'.30 cs 050°T
3 Withy to be left to port	N51°24'.27 E00°33'.37 cs 330°T
4 Withy to be left to port	N51°24'.31 E00°33'.36 cs 340°T
5 Withy to be left to port	N51°24'.34 E00°33'.34 cs 330°T
6 Withy to be left to port	N51°24'.37 E00°33'.31cs 360°T

The channel entrance is approx. 12m W of the West Cardinal in Short Reach.

The course is that following the numbered positions.

At No3, a wide berth is required.

After No6, the entry is made between the barge on the port hand, and the wave baffle wall to starboard.

The co-ordinates are GPS derived, to an estimated accuracy of 3 – 4m.

Courtesy Hoo Marina [2007]

MAIN CHANDLERS	NORTH KENT
Gillingham Marina	173 Pier Road, Gillingham ME7 4LP [*01634* 280022]
Iron Wharf Boatyard	Creek Chandlery, Iron Wharf, Abbeyfields, Faversham ME13 7BY [*01795* 513777]
Pirates Cave Chandlery	Northpoint Business Estate, Unit 14 Enterprise Close Rochester ME2 4LX [*01634* 295233]

SHEERNESS to ROCHESTER YACHT and SAILING CLUBS

Hundred of Hoo Sailing Club
Vicarage Lane, Hoo, Rochester ME3 9LB
01634 250102 / 718779
hundredofhoosc.org.uk
MPA licensed deep water trots and swing moorings,
2 slips, tractors, shore storage
Club house [weekend catering] WC/Shwrs, parking
No allocated visitor berths, but enquire on 01634 718779

Hoo Ness Yacht Club
Vicarage Lane, Hoo, Rochester ME3 9LB
01634 250052 *hooness.org.uk*
About 60 deep water trots, mud berths; 2 slips,
3 scrubbing docks, hoist.
Clubhouse, M/F WCs/Shrs, Bar, Meals to order,
storage ashore, car park
No allocated visitor berths, but enquire on 01634 250311

Kingsferry Boat Club
[Hon. Sec.] 01795 472316
50 half- tide and deep water moorings
[S.E. of Kingsferry Bridge]
Dinghy and car park, water, elec., and slip / cradle.

Lower Halstow Yacht Club
[Hon. Sec.] 01634 324517
lhyc.org.uk
MPA licensed swing moorings; concrete slip, floating jetty,
storage ashore, car park. Club facilities, incl WC/Shwr

Medway Cruising Club
Waterside Lane Gillingham ME7 2SE
medwaycruisingclub.org.uk
Moorings, 2 mooring boats, 3 slips,
2 winches and tractor; jet wash
Club launch ['Invicta' Ch M1 or 37]; dry dock,
dinghy park, storage yard, boatshed
No visitor moorings, but probable availability
Clubhouse, bar, M/F WCs / Shwrs
[Based at Strand Leisure Park, Gillingham]

SHEERNESS to ROCHESTER YACHT and SAILING CLUBS

Medway Yacht Club
Lower Upnor, Rochester ME2 4XB
01634 718399 [office] 718169[clubhouse]
medwayyachtclub.com
Deep water trots, all-tide pontoon, trot and safety boats
storage ashore, car park, library
14t travel hoist, 3t hoist and 3 mast hoists;
scrubbing posts and trolley
Substantial clubhouse, M/F WCs/Shwrs, bar
No visitor berths, but enquire on 01634 718399 [office]

Queenborough Yacht Club
7 High Street, Queenborough ME11 5AA
01795 662051 / 66395
queenboroughyc.co.uk
Clubhouse, bar, WCs/Shwrs [variable opening times],
dinghy park, all-tide short-stay pontoon [elec]
accessing Council swing moorings; weekends'
trot boat in partnership with H.M.

Rochester Cruising Club
10 Esplanade, Rochester ME1 1QN
01634 841350
rochestercc.co.uk
All-tide swing moorings, all-tide pontoon,
scrubbing dock & power wash
Modern clubhouse, WCs/Shwrs, restaurant,
some car parking. Diesel

Royal Engineer Yacht Club
home.sappersailing.org
60 moorings; membership restricted, but discretionary

SEGAS Sailing Club
The Strand, Gillingham, ME7 1TT
seagassailingclub.club
Deep water swing moorings to 11m, slip,
dinghy park, hardstanding
Modern clubhouse. Unrestricted membership

SHEERNESS to ROCHESTER YACHT and SAILING CLUBS

Strood Sailing Club
[above Rochester Bridge]
Temple Manor Marsh, Knight Rd., Strood ME2 2AH
01634 781261
stroodyachtclub.btck.co.uk
Pontoon berths, half - full tide, floating pontoon access, water and elec.,dry dock, crane, car parking; no allocated visitor berths, but enquire
Clubhouse,WC/Shwrs, parking

Upnor Sailing Club
1-3 Pier Place, Lower Upnor, Rochester ME2 4UY
upnorsailing.co.uk
87 full or ½ tide fore and aft moorings, all-tide landing, two ½ tide scrubbing docks; Clubhouse [restricted hours], M/F WCs/Shwrs, secure parking
Sailing cruisers only; no allocation for visitors

Wilsonian Sailing Club
Church Farm, Main Rd., Hoo, Rochester ME3 9HF
01634 250318
wilsoniansc.org.uk
Dinghy sailing, club house with usual facilities; foreshore launching

NORTH KENT DIY YARDS

Mariners Farm Boatyard
391 Lower Rainham Road, Gillingham ME8 7TL 01634 233179
marinersboatyard.co.uk
Mud berths HW +/-2; slip, storage ashore, water and elec, parking; crane and hoist available

Otterham Quay Boatyard
Gillingham ME8 7XE [01634 260250]
crane, storage ashore

Iron Wharf
Abbeyfields, Faversham [01795 537122]
All facilities available

SHEERNESS to ROCHESTER YARDS and MARINAS

Chatham Maritime Marina
Leviathan Way, Chatham Maritime ME4 4LP 01634 899200
mdlmarinas.co.uk
Locked basin with 310 pontoon berths to 24m, water and elec.
Access HW +/- 5;
visitor pontoon off, 20T crane, shore storage, fuel [P&D], M/F WCs/Shwrs, laundromat, MDL WiFi
Adjoining factory outlet shopping, restaurants, PH, convenience store, parking

Gillingham Marina
173 Pier Road, Gillingham ME7 4LP 01634 280022
gillingham-marina.co.uk
Locked basin [2m depth maintained], modern pontoon berths, mostly end-on, but some alongside; water and elec.
Access HW +/- 4½
Tidal basin with modern pontoon berthing. Access HW +/- 3
Deep water visitor berths off. Fuel pontoon access HW +/- 5
20t & 60t hoists, full modern workshop with all trades available
M/F WC / Shwrs, laundromat, cafe, parking, brokerage, chandlery, convenience store 250m

Residential Marine [incorporating Hoo Marina]
Port Werburgh, Vicarage Lane, Rochester ME3 9TW
01634 252107
wanttoliveafloat.com
Marina berthing [residential and short-term], access HW +/-3
Cafe / clubroom, WC/Shwrs, laundromat, 20t cranage, shore storage, boatyard maintenance, chandlery, sailmaker

Whitton Marine
Vicarage Lane, Hoo, Rochester ME3 9LB 01634 250593
whittonmarine.com
Occasional berthing; working slipway, tug, engineering to restoration; marine and brokerage services

Victory Moorings
Admiral's Office, Main Gate, The Historic Dockyard
Chatham ME4 4TZ 07785 971797
Pontoon berthing [all-tide], primarily long term
Access *via* the grounds of the historic dockyard; parking

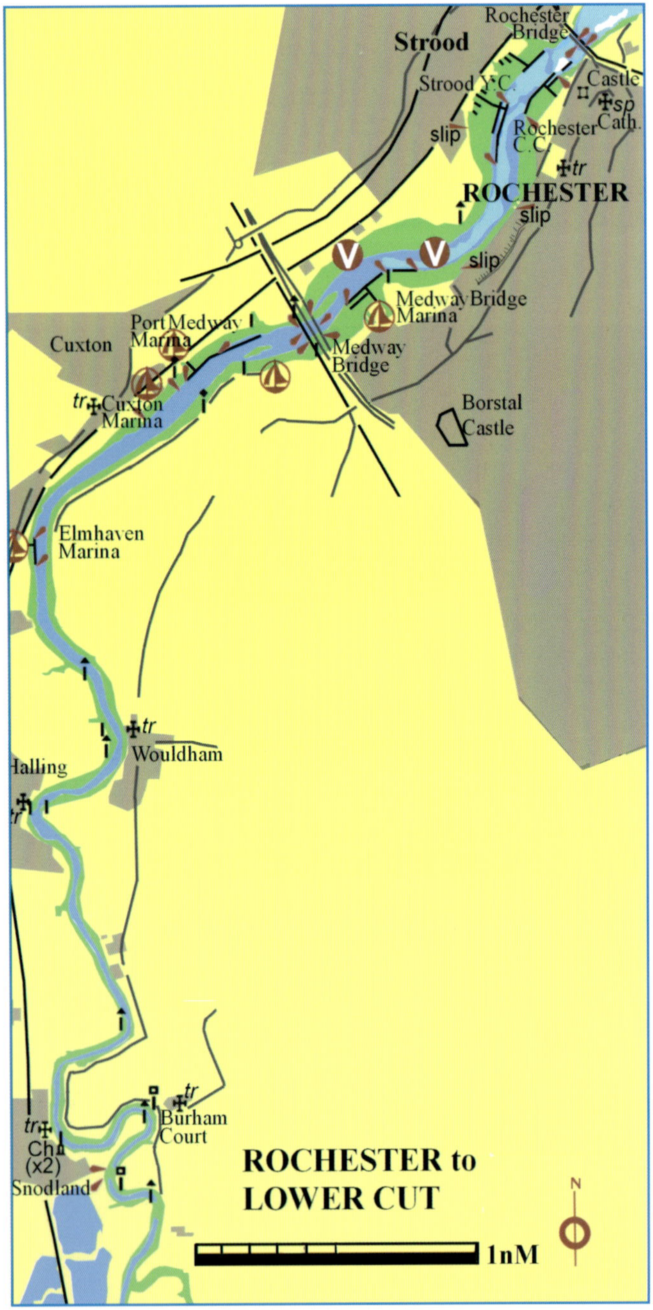

ROCHESTER TO LOWER CUT

The R. Medway

ROCHESTER TO ALLINGTON LOCK

It is difficult now to believe that the upper reaches of the Medway were part of Kent's maritime motorway, but commercial traffic was using it until 2011 when the last freighter served the cement works at Snodland. The absence of commercial traffic can only encourage silting, but the river retains an extraordinary environment of rural, historical, industrial and domestic interest.

The tides seldom exceed 1.5kts. There is a reasonable opportunity to proceed under sail for the first couple of miles, but thereafter power is essential. The river is not buoyed above the bridge, and the few poles with topmarks are mostly on the stbd bank. The few landing places – other than at marinas – are described in the text.

The first obstacle, of course, is Rochester Bridge; traffic generally uses the centre arch, but the Strood arch is also navigable whilst the Rochester arch is not; there is indeed a trifle more water under the Strood arch, but the air draft reduces towards the shore. In terms of the centre arch, Imray & Reeds give the air draft as 5.9m, whilst the Admiralty charts give 5.4m to accord with HAT; local knowledge assumes 5.9m. The centre arch is also lit *[RR, GG, vert]* 24hrs.

UPSTREAM of ROCHESTER BRIDGE

MEDWAY BRIDGE MARINA

HW at Rochester [Strood Pier] is close to that at the Standard Port of Sheerness, where the tidal curve is a near straight line except for the first and last hours. The depths in the immediate vicinity of Rochester Bridge vary rapidly by over a metre, but a charted depth of around 0.5m above datum can be expected at LWS under the bridge, when the air draught will be 11.9m; there is a little less immediately above the bridge, where strong turbulence may be experienced. Above the bridge there are extensive shallows on the Strood shore; at anything less than half-tide, the passage is best made by turning in promptly towards the Rochester Pier, before turning back towards the Strood shore.

There is found on the Strood shore, immediately upstream of the bridge, Jane's Creek which is foul, muddy and of little interest. This is followed by the Pelican YC with its long-term berths with no facilities for visitors, and the Strood YC which is substantial with its clubhouse, shore storage and pontoon berths, but which caters little for visitors.

On the Rochester bank is the Pier – more a pontoon than a pier – with a covered ramp to the Esplanade. This is available for short-term visitors, but the access is security gated and controlled by the Rochester CC; the club is usually open during office hours, and longer during the season, but it is sensible to telephone first [+44 1634 841350]. Above the pier, is the Club's extensive pontoon for reserved berthing.

The published charts are reasonably indicative as to depths, but Wickham Point is to be taken wide to regain the Rochester shore and finding the best water closer to the pontoon of the substantial Medway Bridge Marina; this is immediately before the Medway Bridge, and immediately downstream of the marina is the small and inconspicuous traditional Beacon's boatyard, with mud berthing and basic facilities.

There is relatively little water on the approach to the bridge, and this reach has been known to dry in times of drought. The passage beneath the bridge should be made through the centre span, being aware of the shoaling on the Strood shore; the bridge, with its air draft of 16.7m should present no problems to those having navigated Rochester Bridge.

Above the bridge, there is a small shoal to be avoided whilst turning into Borstal Reach, following which Port Medway and Cuxton Marinas will be found on the stbd hand; both marinas are

The shallows above Rochester Bridge are thought to be occasioned by an historic causeway.

PORT MEDWAY and CUXTON MARINAS

relatively modest but well run, and the best water is found on that bank. There is extensive residential development behind Cuxton Marina, and the charted church tower is inconspicuous behind the green-painted sheds of the marina.

A little above the marina, on the port hand, is an area allocated to water sports; this is marked by a series of small, seasonal buoys. The bend at Cuxton Point should be taken a little wider than the chart suggests, before making for the opposite bank.

Into Clinkham Reach, the small Elmhaven Marina is on the port hand; this is an attractive location, and provides the last facilities before Allington Lock. Upstream, are the walls of an abandoned wharf and, opposite, is the Royal Engineers' Hard; this area is known as the Gunsight.

In Holborough Reach there are further abandoned wharves, and the river from here for a couple of miles is unattractive. Peter's Wharf is one of those abandoned; it served the massive chalk extraction supplying the Snodland cement works, which were last served by river in 2011.

At Wouldham, the depths should be watched, and it is better to favour the stbd hand; 2m of water should be found at half-tide. There is a housing development on the west bank, with steps and pontoon, but both are security gated; there are steps on the

HALLING

There are plans for the excavated area behind Peter's Wharf to be developed with some 5,000 homes served by a new road bridge across the river.

AYLESFORD PRIORY - 'THE FRIARS'

opposite bank, suggestive of an historic causeway. At Halling, the charted church tower is inconspicuous, being largely obscured by modern housing.

A modern trading estate precedes the commencement of Reeds Paper Mills, identified by the huge stocks of recycling material; the mills extend for a half-mile or so on and behind both banks, with the river spanned by a high level gantry. The river then turns into a series of tight bends and at N00°19.5 there are shallows on the bend at the old wharf; otherwise, better than 2m of water should be found at half-tide. The 'Hawkwood Stone' is above the east bank; upstream from here until Allington Lock, anchoring is prohibited other than in an emergency, because of the numerous cables and service pipes on the river bed which, anyway, is stoney.

On the east bank is the 'Hawkwood Stone', marking the limit of the jurisdiction of the 'Admiral of the Medway'. This is now an honorary mayoral title.

BURHAM MARSHES

The Lower, Middle and Upper Cuts facilitated traffic serving the industrial area of East Hythe, following which the environment reverts to the rural, with the Friary on the port hand. At about E000°28.6, a little before Aylesford, there will be found a quiet wharf on the stbd bank which is useful for a short stay; about 1.5m of water will be found from ¾ tide; there are iron bollards [but these have no caps, and lines need to be watched as the level rises]; there is a public footpath leading to a nearby PH.

Aylesford Bridge merits attention, with its air draft of 2.8m and a depth of 4.75m at HWS [that is, 7.5m between river bed and the underside of the arch, as measured in September 2012]; it is not only a matter of clearance when passing upstream on a rising tide, but ensuring also a sufficient clearance when returning. Immediately below the bridge, on the stbd bank, is a permanent ladder leading to public open space but a dinghy would be needed for access; on the opposite bank is The Chequers PH with river terrace. The bridge is now limited to pedestrians, and the road bridge is a little upstream with an air draft of 3.2m and a similar depth of water.

Above Aylesford, the environment is rural with at least a similar level of water maintained; a lookout must be kept however, for the large amount of floating vegetation which can include some general debris; it seems to be captured in this length, and the banks should be left well clear.

The M2 road bridge has an air draft of 9.4m; a little above, on the stbd bank is a small boatyard with few facilities and used primarily for long-term DIY maintenance.

The approach to Allington Lock is undemanding, and is made from the stbd side of the river; the lock is maintained by the Environment Agency, and operated *only* by their staff. All craft using the lock, and navigating upstream, must be licensed by the Agency; registration is available with the lock office, and is chargeable by boat length and duration of navigation; the charges are modest – typically £10 per day.

AYLESFORD BRIDGE

The Friars was the extensive Dominican Priory created in the 15th century, and dissolved at the Reformation when it passed into private hands. It was repurchased by the Dominicans in 1951, and remains an active and beautifully maintained centre.

This modern lock accommodates vessels of up to 53m length and 6m beam. It is manned 24hrs, from HW-0300 to HW+0200, between 1 March and 31 October, where those hours fall between 0700hrs and sunset [otherwise between 0800hrs and 1600hrs]; outside those hours, it is manned on 24hrs notice [01622 752864]. The facilities include a waiting pontoon, overnight berthing, WC/showers, chemical toilet disposal and pump-out, and garbage disposal.

The river is still navigable upstream from Allington Lock - accepting the limited air draught - and thence through Maidstone and on through Tonbridge. The Agency endeavours to maintain 2m depth until Maidstone, but there are no longer any public WCs or similar facilities on that length.

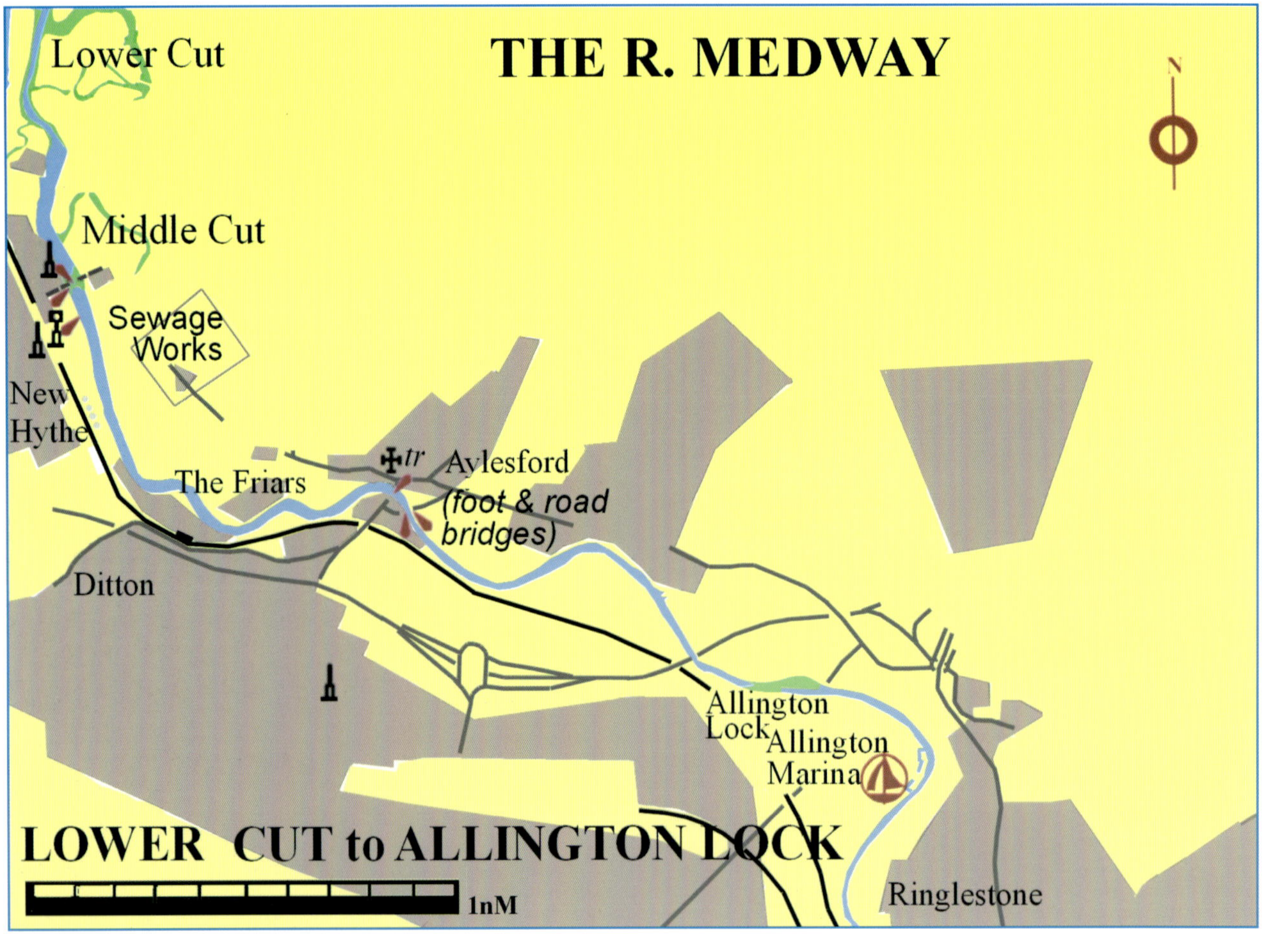

LOWER CUT TO ALLINGTON LOCK

ALLINGTON LOCK

DEBRIS ABOVE AYLESFORD BRIDGE

ROCHESTER to ALLINGTON LOCK MARITIME INFORMATION

CHARTS Admiralty 1834, SC5606.4
Imray 2100.3,4, Y18, C1

TIDAL DIFFERENCES on SHEERNESS [approx]
Rochester [Strood Pier] +0020
Allington Lock +0050

COASTGUARD THAMES [Thames Coastguard Ch 16 67]
[*01255* 675518]

NAVIGATION AUTHORITY Medway Ports [969645]
Medway Ports Navigation Service [to Allington Lock]
[Medway VTS Ch74] [663025]

Speed limit 6kts
Environment Agency [Allington Lock and Upstream]
[*01622* 752864]
[Lock Operational HW -3 to HW+2; daylight hours,
& other times by application]
Max beam 6m, waiting pontoon, slip, WCs, Shwrs,
pump-out
Environment Agency [River License] [*08708* 506506]
or license available at lock

ROCHESTER BRIDGE Centre arch clearance at HAT: 5.4m
at MHWS: 5.9m

AYLESFORD BRIDGE
Centre arch clearance at MHWS: 2.4 m approx

CLUB
Rochester CC, 10 The Esplanade, Rochester ME1 1QN
[841350] Clubhouse with bar, meals, WCs / shwrs.
Pontoon berths with water / elec/ TV; diesel

STD CODE 01634 ***unless shown otherwise***

ROCHESTER to ALLINGTON LOCK MARINA BERTHING

Port Medway Marina
Station Road, Cuxton, Rochester ME2 1AB [720033]
Pontoon and drying berths, water, elec, fuel,
lift out and shore storage
Tug, most maintenance, brokerage, WCs, Shwrs

Cuxton Marina
Pontoon and drying berths, water, elec, fuel,
lift out and shore storage
Most maintenance, brokerage, WCs, Shwrs

Beacon Boatyard
Manor Lane, Rochester MA1 3JN [841320]
Tidal berthing, lift out, store storage, most maintenance
WCs, Shwrs, Brokerage, Marine surveys

Medway Bridge Marina
Manor Lane, Rochester ME1 3HS [843576]
Pontoon and drying berths, water, elec, fuel,
lift out and shore storage
Most maintenance, brokerage, WCs, Shwrs, Cafe

Elmhaven Marina
Rochester Road, Halling, ME2 1AQ [240489]
Tidal pontoon berthing [HW+/-41/2], water, elec, slip,
Marine engineer, canvas work on site, brokerage, WC, Shwr

STD CODE 01634 ***unless shown otherwise***

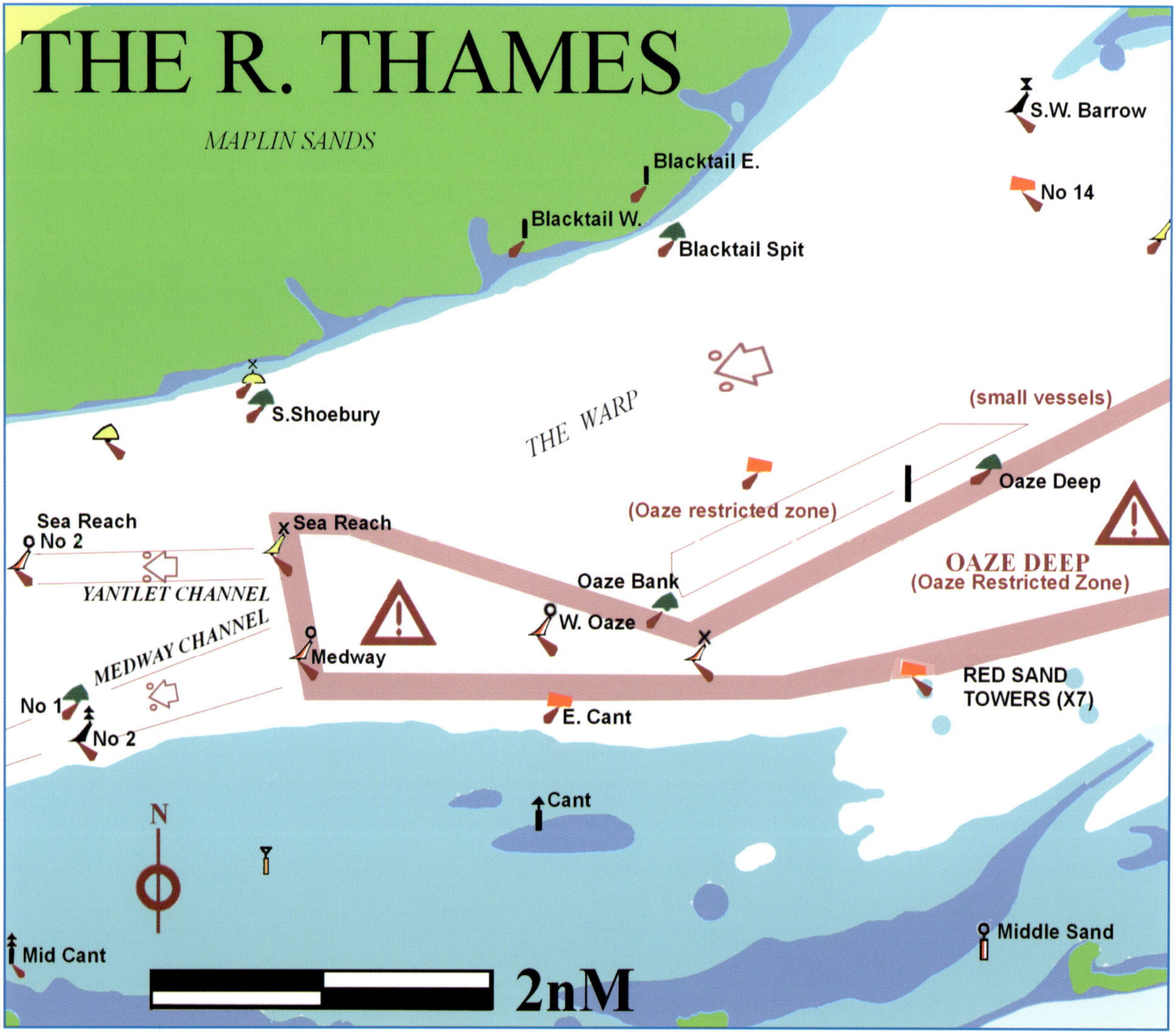

OAZE to YANTLET CHANNEL

The R. Thames

OAZE TO DARTFORD CREEK

The lower reaches of the Kentish Thames extend some 30nM; this must be the most boring section of the River, but it is a necessary passage to attain the upper reaches! There are few challenges, given an awareness of large vessels in the main channel and the numerous tugs, lighters and workboats operating outside the channel. Weather conditions can be robust, with little protection from the low-lying agricultural areas to the south; with the numerous bends, sailing conditions can be 'flukey'.

The Thames is not subject to any formal speed limit; there is a recommended limit of 10kts in Gravesend Reach and above, and an 8kts limit on broadcast occasions in the vicinity of vessels moored or working close to the navigation channel.

The main channel is well buoyed, but the extensive mud flats are not well defined. There are numerous opportunities for anchoring, but few are comfortably free from the wash of large vessels. There are no landings for small craft above Queenborough or Southend-on-Sea and below Gravesend, other than at the Allhallows SC and Thurrock YC.

The Port of London Authority [PLA] publishes a useful 'Tidal Thames Recreational Users Guide' [www.pla.co.uk / PLA, Gravesend DA12 2BG / 01474 562200].

Weather

The Thames Estuary is very exposed and, combined with the shallow waters, severe conditions may be encountered and there is a significant risk of fog; if fog is encountered, it is best to anchor well out outside any commercial channel and to advise Thames Coastguard of the situation.

At the risk of sounding both repetitious and pompous, a passage plan for more than perhaps a three hours' excursion should look not only to the day's forecast, but also to the three days'. The conditions can vary widely over a relatively small area; it is not unknown for there to be a F3 and a calm sea at Walton-on-the-Naze, with a F5 and 1m waves in the Edinburgh Channel; the more severe conditions will extend the passage time and, particularly if the destination is tide-dependent, it is worthwhile 'phoning ahead to check the local conditions.

A passage in the outer part of the estuary may well provide the first experience of sailing out of sight of land.

Tides

The Standard Port is Tilbury but, for the lower reaches, comparison should be made with Sheerness, particularly for the tidal curve. The tidal streams in the Thames are usually within 2kts, but occasionally achieve 4kts; the tidal range is up to 7m, and slack mooring lines are to be avoided.

Navigation

The approach from the north is best made by holding the Essex coast until west of Southend-on-Sea; there is an 8kts speed limit inshore. Inbound craft should make a southwesterly course to *W. Leigh Middle [QG]*, and then cross the Yantlet Channel to *E. Blyth [Fl(2)R 10s]*; outbound craft should defer crossing until after *Sea Reach No5. [Iso 5s]*; the southern small craft traffic is accordingly two-way between *Sea Reach No4 [FlY 2.5s]* and *Sea Reach No7 [FlY 2.5s]*. The approach from the east – the north Kent coast - best avoids commercial traffic by taking the Overland Passage, clearing Cheyney Spit and Jacob's Bank, and making towards *W. Cant [QR]* before heading due north to cross the Medway Approach Channel to *Grain Edge [unlit]* and thence into the Swatchway.

The extent of Grain Spit should not be underestimated. If

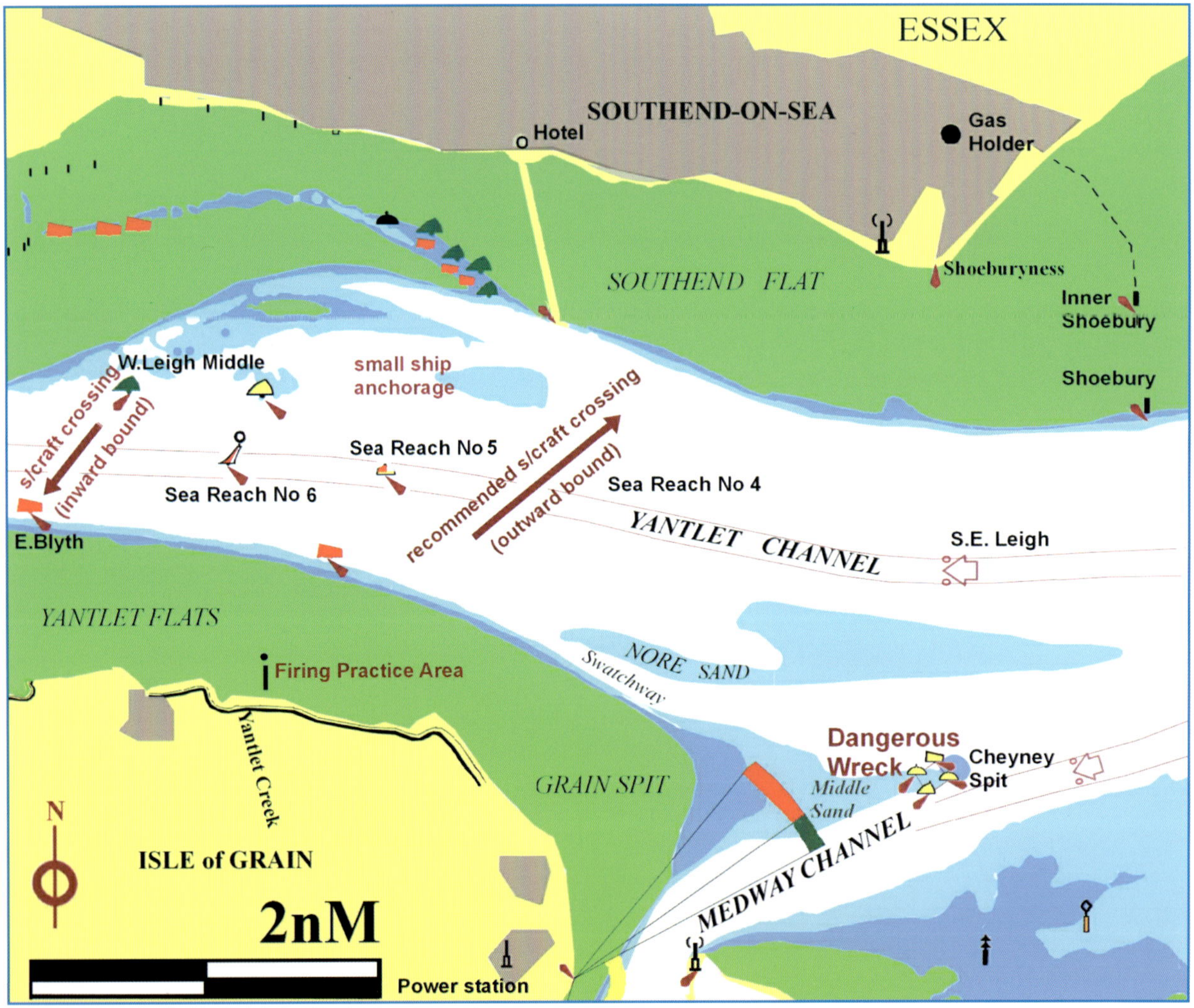

THE YANTLET CHANNEL

passaging between the Thames and the Medway, it can be only marginally advantageous to arrive at Grain Spit at low water, as this can add another 4-5nM to the passage; a shoal-draught craft on the ebb would best make the Spit with better than a quarter tide in hand, to enable a comfortable crossing of the Sheerness Middle Sand.

The north-eastern shore of Grain Spit is occupied by the Yantlet Demolition area, and is marked by a series of yellow buoys [unlit], and extending upstream to the entrance to Yantlet Creek; landing is not permitted. Yantlet Creek dries, runs for about 1nM, and is of little interest except as a possible anchorage; the approach channel across the flats is ill-defined and, from the Swatchway, the beacon should be approached on about 215°T for 0.2nM, followed by a port hand bend and a continuation for about a further 0.2nM on about 170°T; the port hand banks have extensive mud flats, but the stbd hand banks are steeper-to. There is more water in the creek at LW than in the river; there is road access at the bridge.

Upstream of the creek is the village of Allhallows, with its sailing club. The Yantlet Flats continue into the Blyth Sands, where both St. Mary's Bay and Egypt Bay have seabed cables crossing the river; anchoring in the vicinity is prohibited. The channel narrows on the approach to Lower Hope Point and care must be taken if there is any traffic in the offing; at low water, there is very little outside the channel. Within Lower Hope Reach is Cliffe Creek, a small drying creek of little interest; above, is the Alpha jetty handling sand and ballast; behind, there is a ruined fortification and a land-locked dinghy club.

THURROCK YC

Whilst most small craft will so far have maintained the south [Kentish] shore, between ***Lower Hope** [FlR 5s]* and ***Mucking** 7 [FlG 5s]* inbound craft should cross to the north [Essex] shore, leaving the south shore to outbound craft; small craft are not excluded from the main channel, subject to the usual precautions. There is no compulsion to these directions, but they make for better traffic management and avoidance of the Shellhaven Wharf.

The course should be just outside the main channel at ***Mucking** 5* and ***Mucking** 7,* and taking the bend wide into Gravesend Reach to avoid any tidal set onto the flats; from here onwards, a speed limit of 10kts is recommended. In Gravesend

DARTFORD BRIDGE

There is progressive removal of the centre channel buoyage in the Yantlet Channel, to better accommodate very large vessels; commercial traffic will be encountered in the secondary channels, which extend to approx 130m both sides of the main channel, from Sea Reach 1 to the Shellhaven jetty.

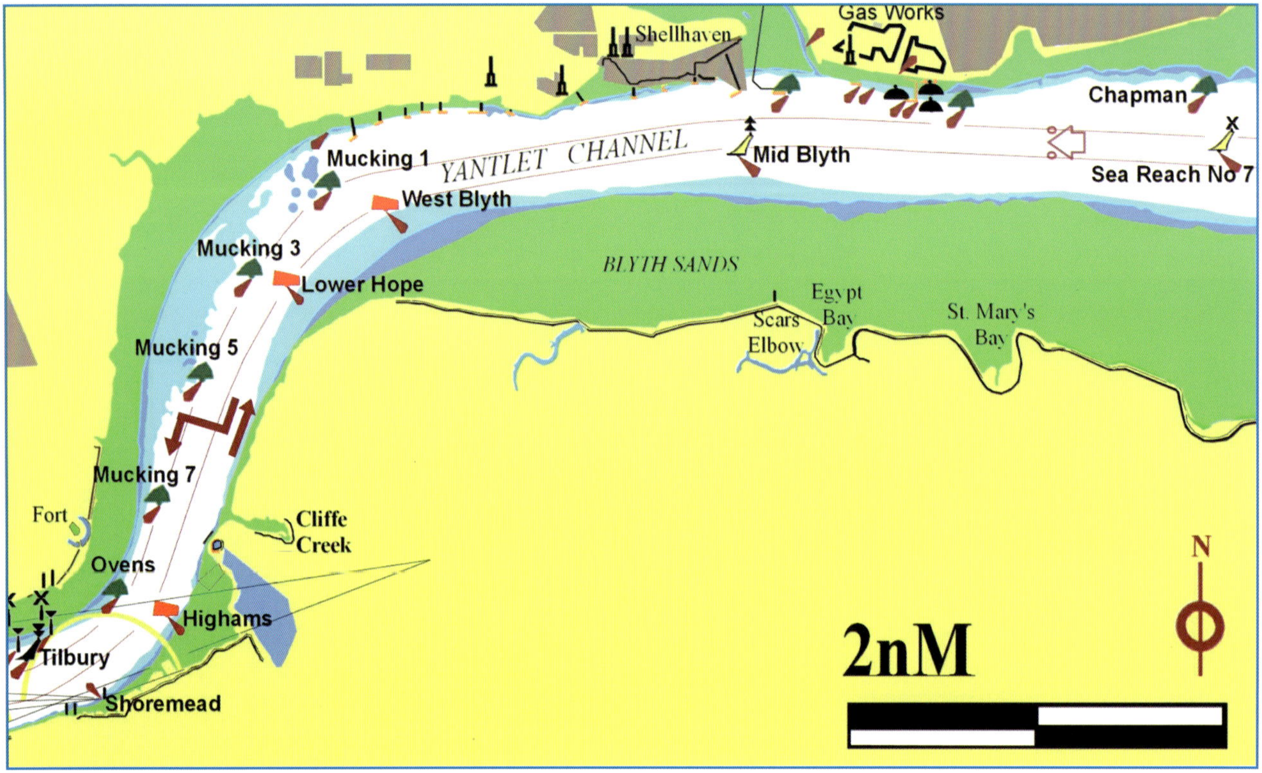

YANTLET CHANNEL TO QUEENS REACH

THE ENTRANCE TO DARTFORD CREEK

Reach there is a series of beacons to be left to stbd; there is little sea room between the main channel and the London Cruise Terminal followed by the cargo jetty, before the turn into Northfleet Hope and the entrance to Tilbury docks. The Tilbury lock poses particular problems for large vessels when manoeuvring; the river here is narrow, with strong tidal sets and a blind bend. Upstream, and immediately below *White Hart [FlG 5s]*, is the substantial Thurrock YC [01375 373720] with its small craft moorings.

On the bend – opposite Broadness - into Fiddler's Reach there is again little water between the channel and the steep-to mud bank of Black Shelf. The bend at Stone Ness should be taken quite wide; there is otherwise plenty of water, but it is necessary to remain alert for commercial traffic; at the

The PLA recommends that a suitable anchor is to hand, with a minimum of 5m chain and 25m rope.

oil terminal immediately below the Queen Elizabeth Bridge, vessels should keep about 60m off the jetty; a compulsory speed limit for this section may be broadcast on occasions. The passage under the bridge should be made quite close-in to the base pier.

DARTFORD CREEK

Returning downstream, Dartford Creek marks the county boundary. Dartford Creek, the entrance to the River Darent and its tributary the River Cray, served Dartford and Crayford for centuries. The tidal barrier at the entrance was constructed in 1981 as part of the Thames Barrier system of protective embankments; the barrier has been overhauled and is again fully operational. It is managed by the Thames Barrier Team of the Environment Agency, and is closed when HWS Sheerness exceeds 3.4m.

The barrier has an air draught of 11m [when open], and the

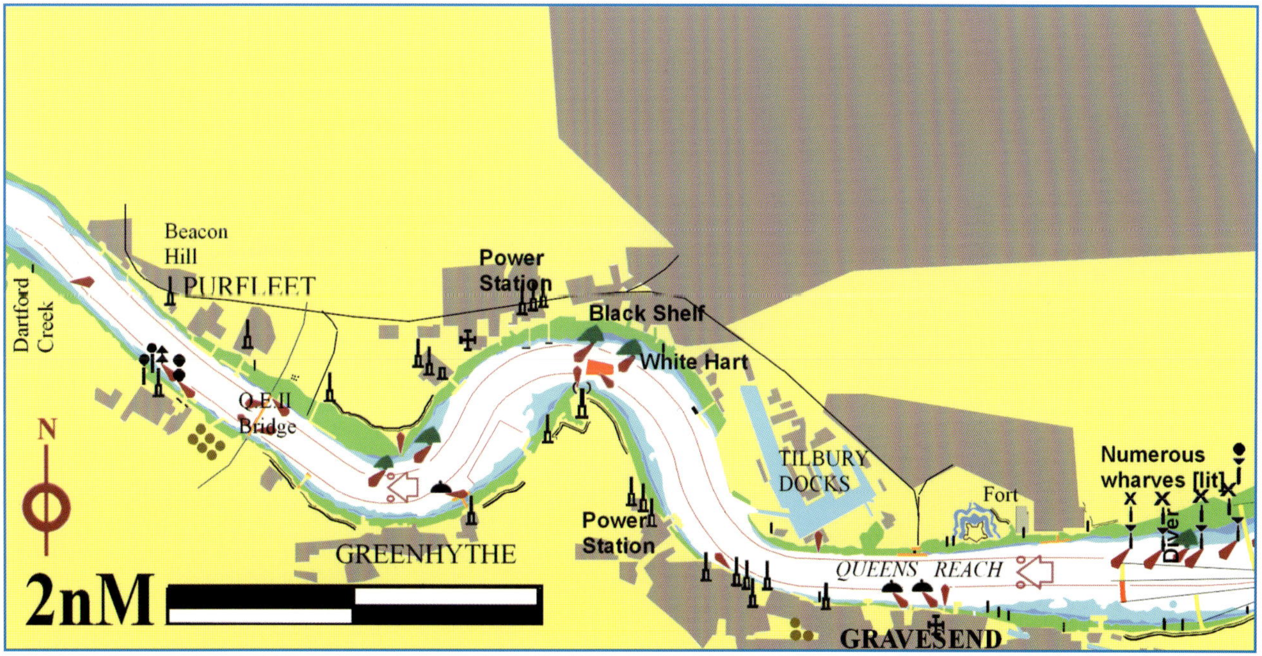

QUEENS REACH TO DARTFORD CREEK

Yachtsmen are reminded that there is no fuel provision before Tower Bridge, other than at Gravesend; this however, has limited access.

approach dries 3m above CD. There is little published pilotage, but there is a speed limit of 8kts within the creek, and local knowledge suggests better than 2m depth at HWS; the road bridge at 1.5m, in the town approach, has an air draught of only about 2m.

The pastoral settings is surprisingly attractive, but there are no public landing places.

Downstream from the creek, there is a mile or so of agricultural land behind the flood defences, before 'Littlebrook D' power station with its landmark single chimney. There is a couple more jetties and, standing well off, guides the passage through the centre span of the Queen Elizabeth II Bridge; this should be made close to the pier, and there is little water between the 2m contour and the main channel. Immediately downstream is the busy Thames Europort; the turn past Greenhithe finds plenty of water and on the shoreline modern residential development gives way to the sea wall protecting the Swanscombe Marshes with the tall electricity pylon close to the shoreline; the foreshore below the flats is foul ground. Immediately above Broadness is Broadness Creek, with its unpleasant ambience; this is a drying creek which extends for about a half-mile, with various mud berths with no facilities or ready road access. Entry to the creek requires avoidance of the shoal guarding its upstream shore.

At the Ness, there is less than a ¼ cable between the 5m contour and the main channel; strong turbulence may be experienced as well as wind shifts. There is little room here for the manoeuvring commercial vessels with their attendant tugs, and the abandoned White's Jetty should be left well clear. Immediately downstream of the Ness is the Seacon wharf and transit shed, and this too is busy; this is opposite the lock to Tilbury Docks, in Gravesend Reach.

Immediately above Gravesend is a series of commercial wharves to be left well clear, continuing to Gravesend Embankment, and this has been much improved in recent years. The Royal Terrace Pier is used by the Thames Navigation Service and is inaccessible to the yachtsman; the West Street Pier is used by the Gravesend-Tilbury ferry, which is busy and similarly inaccessible; there are also two small basins of little practical importance, although one could run up onto the hard in desperation. Immediately below the pier is the white-painted building of the

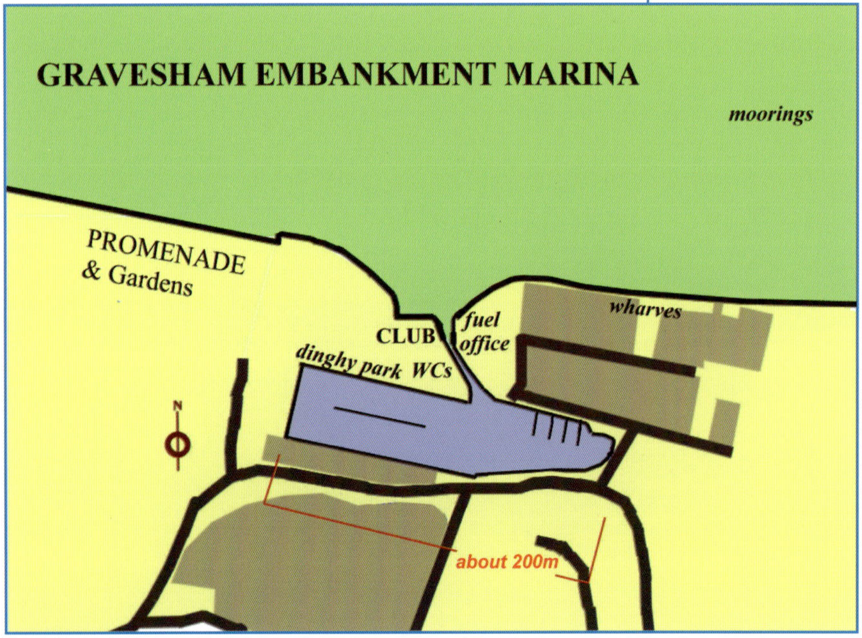

GRAVESHAM MARINA

The PLA reminds yachtsmen that, above Denton Wharf, the Thames is a 'Category C' waterway, where wave heights of 1.2m and tidal flows of up to 4kts may be encountered.

THE ENTRANCE to GRAVESHAM MARINA

DENTON WHARF

Gravesend Rowing Club; off this, is the unsecured 'Newbridge' wooden jetty and steps.

The entrance to Gravesend Embankment Marina is narrow and inconspicuous, but identifiable by the Gravesend SC building on the entrance wharf and the long office building to the rear. The single lock gate is open only at free flow – about HW +/- 1, and the depth in the basin can fall to less than 1m; the entrance channel can move a little. The marina is too small to justify the cost of new locks, but together with the Gravesend SC has a very friendly atmosphere. Diesel is available at about HW +/-2 hrs during working hours, without having to enter the basin.

The approaches are well described by the Gravesend SC as

'When arriving from seaward, keep just outside (either to north or south) of the buoyed deep water channel down Lower Hope Reach and round Coalhouse Point. On the north shore there are a number of groynes marked by green posts with topmarks; if keeping to the north side of the river leave these to starboard (there is a row of buoys just before the groynes to discourage passing between the posts and the shore - not a good idea except at high water). On the south shore the landscape will change from marsh to a long gravel jetty, then moored commercial craft. At the end of the groynes is Tilbury power station, distinguished by two tall chimneys. When almost past the power station turn towards the south shore, keeping a good lookout for large commercial traffic. Identify the last of the tug and larger commercial craft moorings ahead of you, and leave these to port. The tide can run up to 4 knots - head well uptide of moored craft. Once into the moorings head towards the shore. Ahead of you will be the Gordon Promenade with some grass, and the café in the background. At the left-hand (eastern) end of the promenade Gravesend Sailing Club is visible, a low building with a varnished frontage onto the river, white ends, and black roof, distinguished by a flagpole in front of the Clubhouse and a large sign along the front of the Clubhouse.

As a guide, there is about 2m depth on the outer small craft moorings at low tide. Immediately to the left (east) of the Clubhouse is the entrance to the Canal Basin. There is a (relatively) deep water channel whose position changes from time to time. If possible it's best to inspect at low water; if going in at half-tide (when the mud each side of the channel is visible) keep slightly to the west of the channel centreline. If no mud is visible, head due south towards the lifebelt on the shore and line up the lifebelt with the middle of a row of three or four short trees - a bearing of 175ET. Head in on this bearing. Turn to port when the lock gates are half obscured by the upriver knuckle and head straight for the right-hand edge of the entrance. (We usually have a small pontoon or buoy moored off the front of the Clubhouse - if so, leave that close to starboard).

If the gates to the basin are closed its best to moor in the entrance, against the right-hand wall. Moor as close to the swing bridge as possible to leave the cranes clear. Be on guard for wash from passing vessels, use plenty of fenders, and allow for the rise and fall of the tide.

There is a row of large yellow mooring buoys just off, with stout pick-up strops; they are available for general use [at a modest charge] and replace the old PLA seaplane moorings. Downstream are the moorings of the Gravesend Sailing Club; these are freely available for a short stay, but few have strops, and those inshore have little water; only one is dedicated to visitors.

At the lower end of the Reach is another commercial wharf, and Denton Wharf also; Denton Wharf is the PLA maintenance yard, which accepts commercial commissions, but more as engineers than shipwrights. The bend into Lower Hope Reach is marked by the ruins of Shornmead Fort, and Higham Bight – above the Alpha Jetty – provides a recognised anchorage with good holding in mud.

In Lower Hope Reach, inbound small craft will again be encountered before their turn for the Essex shore.

THE RIVER THAMES: OAZE to DARTFORD CREEK — MARITIME INFORMATION

CHARTS Admiralty 1186; SC5606 8-14; Imray 2100, C1, C2

TIDAL DIFFERENCES on HW LONDON BRIDGE
Gravesend 0050; Dartford Creek -0045

NAVIGATION AUTHORITY Port of London Authority
Royal Pier Road, Gravesend DA12 2BG
[*01474* 562362 (Admin)]
[*01474* 562333 (Operations)]
VHF: ['London VTS'] Inwards to Sea Reach No4 Ch68, 18;
Sea Reach No4 to Crayfordness Ch 14, 22
['Thames Patrol'] Ch 69, 14, 68, 16

COASTGUARD
Thames Coastguard [seaward of Canvey Island]
London Coastguard [above Canvey Island]
Ch 16, 67 [*01255* 675518]

MARINA BERTHING Embankment Marina, Canal Basin
Albion Parade, Gravesend DA12 2RN [*01474* 535700]
Locked access HW+/-1, pontoon berths [water and elec],
basin moorings [limited depth]
Lift-out, limited shore storage, diesel [HW+/-2],
Pump-out, Calor, WCs/Shwrs

REPAIRS and MAINTENANCE
Enquire of Gravesham Marina or PLA

STD CODE 01227 ***unless shown otherwise***

THE RIVER THAMES: OAZE to DARTFORD CREEK — TOWN INFORMATION

TRANSPORT

Rail	Gravesend [1M]
Buses	Arriva [*0844* 8004411]
Local	Traveline [*0871* 2002233]
Taxis	Gravesend Taxis [*01634* 566570]
	Walkers Cars [*01474* 560666]

POLICE Non emergency [101]

HOSPITAL [A&E] Medway Hospital [830000]
Doctor Downs Way Medical Practice
Worcester Close, Gravesend DA13 9LB [*0844* 8151333]
Dentist Gravesend Dental Surgery
79 Leander Drive, Gravesend DA12 4NF [*01474* 352990]

SHOPPING
Adequate general shopping in Town Centre [½ M]

PHs and Restaurants Limited choice

CLUBS

Thurrock YC
Argent Street, Grays RM17 6JF
VHF Ch M [*01375* 373720]
Deep water moorings and mud berths;
clubhouse with most facilities

Gravesend SC
Promenade East, Gravesend DA12 2RN
[*07538* 326623 (Clubhouse)]
[*07506* 367699 (Duty Officer)]
www.gravesendsc.org.uk
All-tide moorings [some for visitors];
club house with most facilities

STD CODE 01227 ***unless shown otherwise***

Appendix I

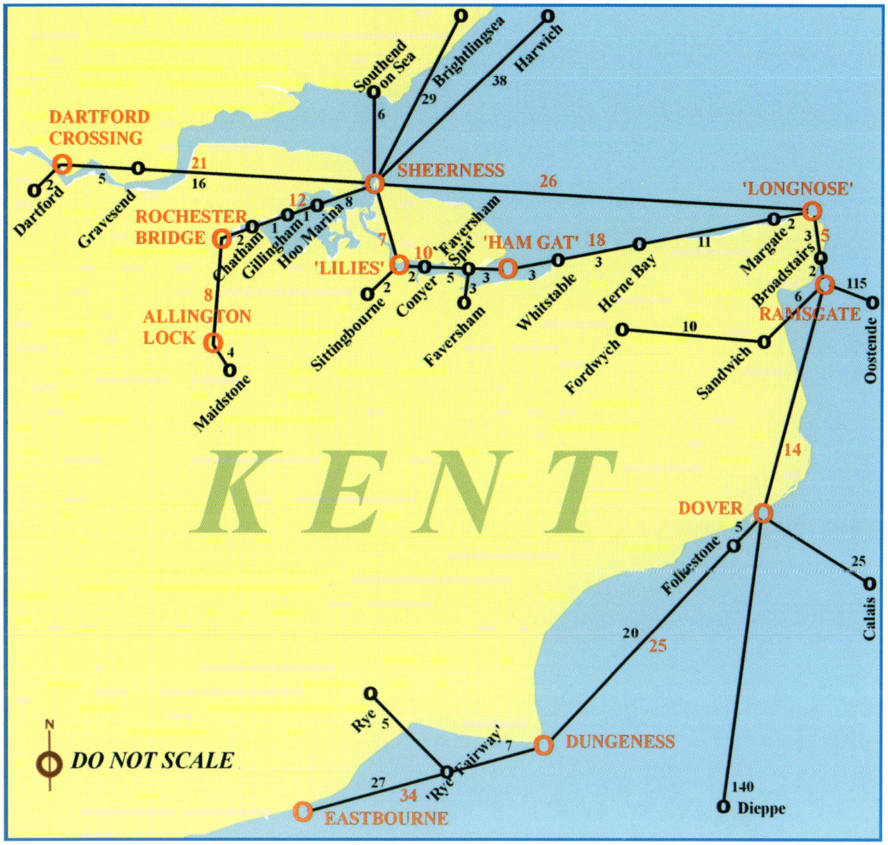

DISTANCES' CHART NOTES

The distances shown are approximate, and in nautical miles for the shortest navigable passage. They may well be tide dependent, and this is obviously so in the cases of drying harbours.

The distances between the waypoints are not to scale. Some of the lesser waypoints are 'off track', and accordingly the distances shown are on the limits of reasonable accuracy.

It is the navigator's responsibility to check distances against published charts and tide tables, and to decide on the feasibility of the proposed passage.

Appendix II

APPROXIMATE TIDAL DIFFERENCES

Note – The Standard Port for Margate, Herne Bay, Whitstable, Faversham and Conyer is given as Sheerness, but local knowledge generally bases predictions on Dover and are based on observation.

STANDARD PORT	LOCATION		HW	LW
Shoreham-on-Sea	Eastbourne	Sovereign Hbr Safe Water mark	+0010	+0020
Dover	Rye	Rye Harbour	-0010	Dries
	Folkestone	Folkestone Harbour ent.	-0010	Dries
	Sandwich	Town Quay	+0030	+0030
	Ramsgate	Ramsgate Harbour ent.	+0015	+0015
	Broadstairs	Pierhead	+0020	+0020
	Faversham	Town Quay	+0125	Creek Dries
	Conyer	Swale Marina	+0125	Creek Dries
Sheerness	Margate	Margate Harbour	-0045	Dries
	Herne Bay	Herne Bay Harbour ent.	-0020	Dries
	Whitstable	Whitstable Harbour ent.	-0010	Dries
	Faversham	Town Quay	+0250	Dries
	Conyer	Swale Marina	+0250	Creek Dries
	Queenborough	All-tide Landing	0000	0000
	Halstow Creek	Head of Creek	+ 0010	Creek Dries
	Gillingham	Gillingham Marina	+0010	+0010
	Hoo	Hoo Marina	+0015	+0015
	Chatham	Chatham Marina	+0010	+0010
	Rochester	Strood Pier	+0020	+0020
	Allington Lock	Lock Entrance	+0050	Varies
London Bridge	Gravesend	Gravesend Basin	-0050	Entrance Dries
	Dartford	Dartford Creek	-0045	Entrance Dries

APPROXIMATE TIDAL DIFFERENCES AMONG STANDARD PORTS and DOVER

Note – The differences in both tables are approximate, and for the purpose of initial passage planning only.

STANDARD PORT	AVERAGE DIFFERENCE	PROBABLE MAXIMUM DEVIATION from AVERAGE	
		HW	LW
Shoreham	+0005	+0025	-0025
Sheerness	+0125	+0035	-0015
London Bridge	+0225	+0045	-0030
Walton-on-the-Naze	+0030	+0030	-0040

Appendix II continued

TIDAL STREAMS Based on HW Dover

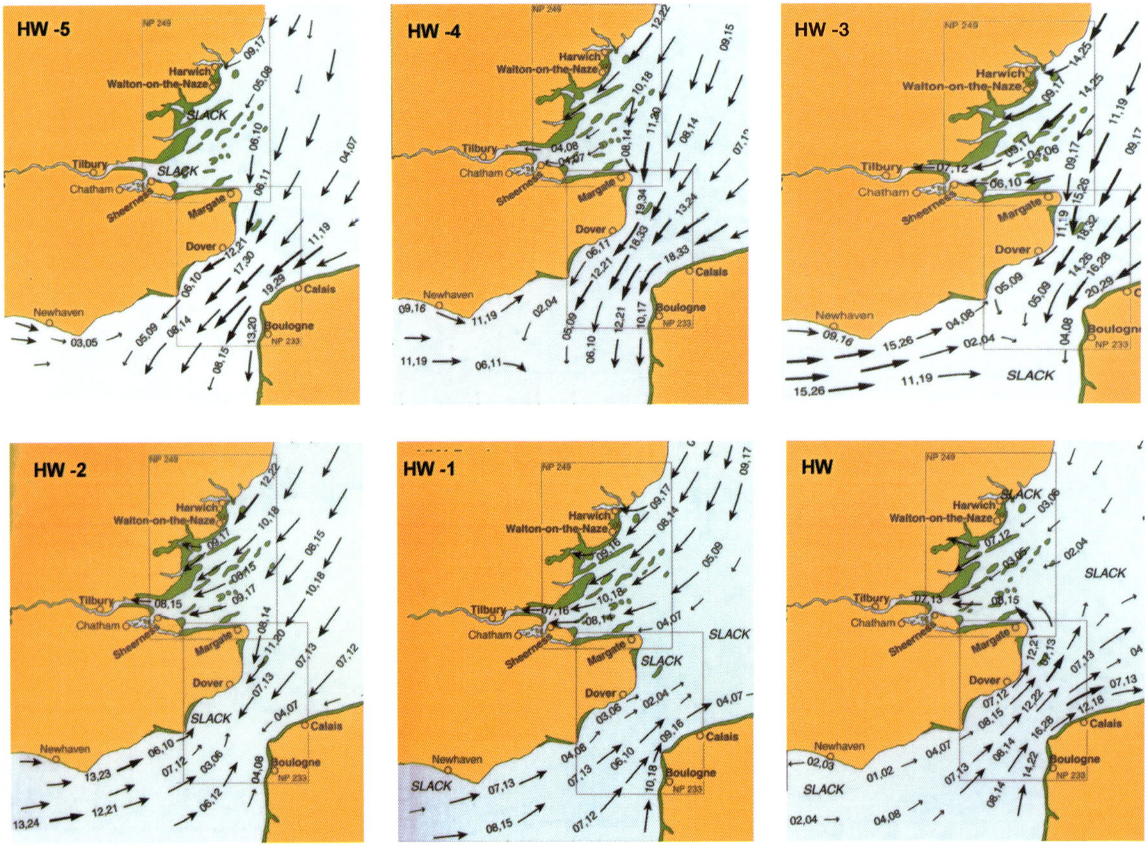

HW+1
NP 249
Harwich
Walton-on-the-Naze
SLACK
Tilbury
SLACK
Chatham
Sheerness
Margate
Dover
Calais
Newhaven
Boulogne
NP 233
SLACK

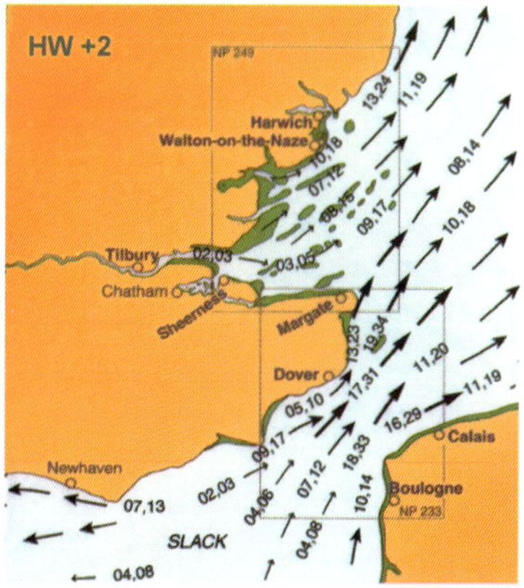
HW +2
NP 249
Harwich
Walton-on-the-Naze
Tilbury
Chatham
Sheerness
Margate
Dover
Calais
Newhaven
Boulogne
NP 233
SLACK

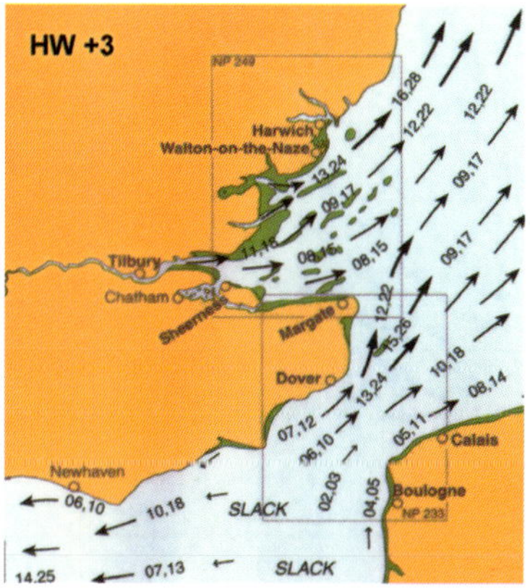
HW +3
NP 249
Harwich
Walton-on-the-Naze
Tilbury
Chatham
Sheerness
Margate
Dover
Calais
Newhaven
SLACK
Boulogne
NP 233
SLACK

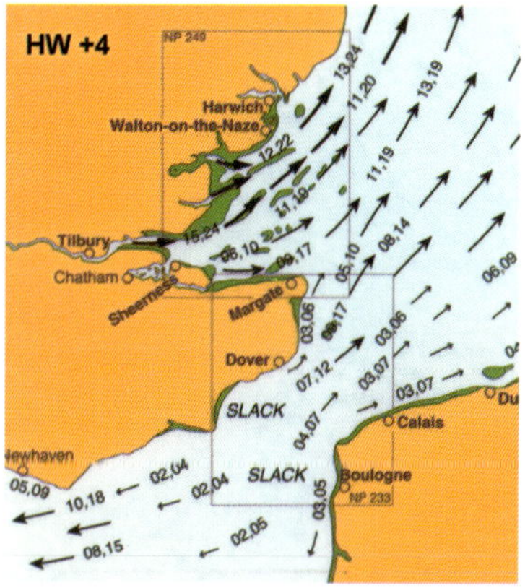
HW +4
NP 249
Harwich
Walton-on-the-Naze
Tilbury
Chatham
Sheerness
Margate
Dover
SLACK
Calais
Newhaven
SLACK
Boulogne
NP 233

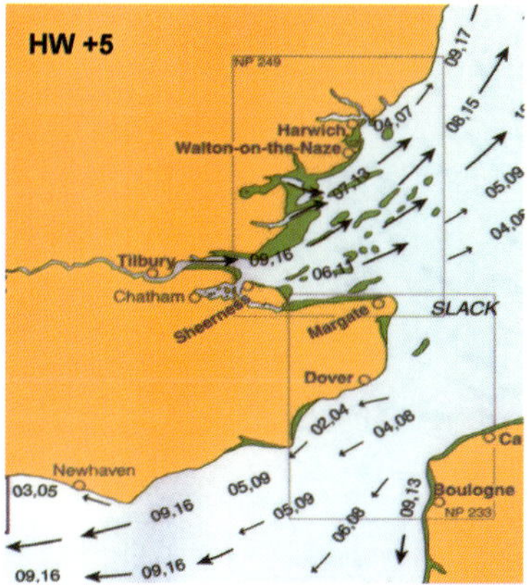
HW +5
NP 249
Harwich
Walton-on-the-Naze
Tilbury
Chatham
Sheerness
Margate
SLACK
Dover
Newhaven
Boulogne
NP 233

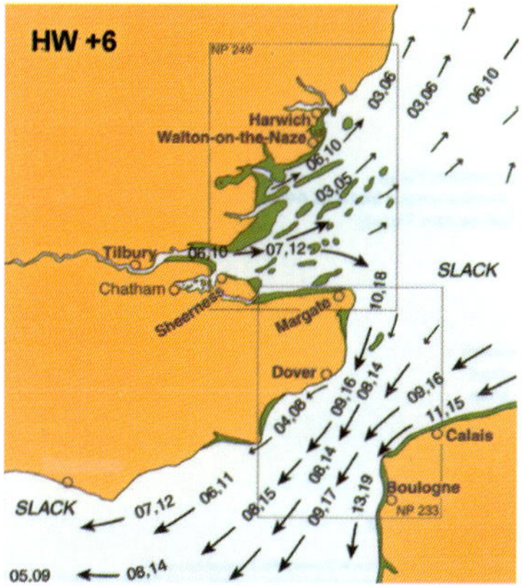
HW +6
NP 249
Harwich
Walton-on-the-Naze
Tilbury
Chatham
SLACK
Sheerness
Margate
Dover
Calais
SLACK
Boulogne
NP 233

Appendix II continued

TIDAL CURVES

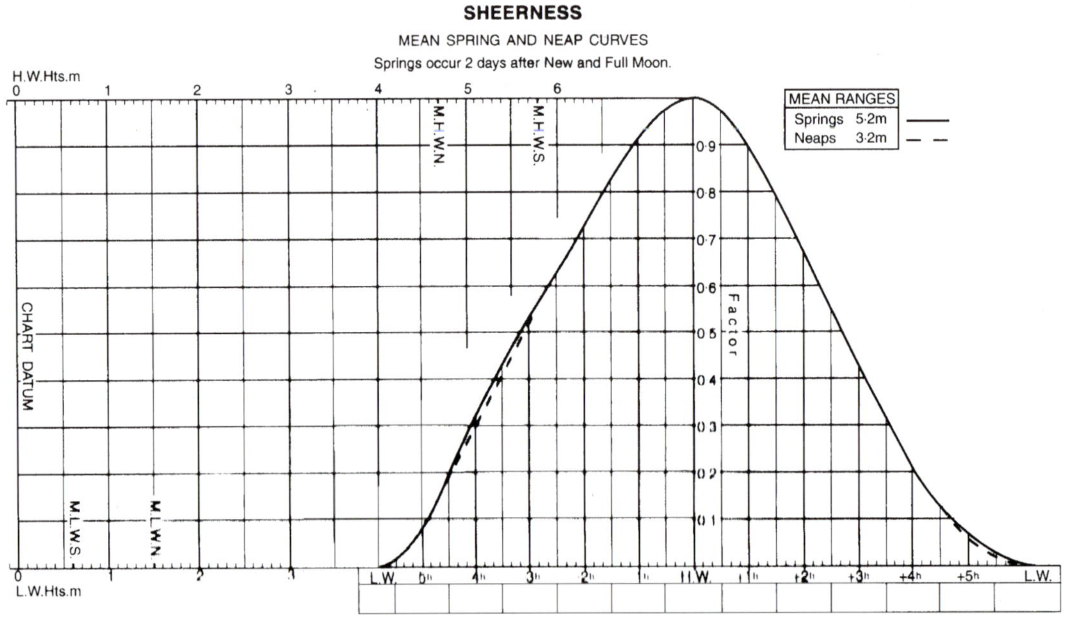

Tidal predictions should be treated with caution. A combination of barometric pressure, wind, floodwater and downstream tidal surge can cause a difference of a metre or more.

DOVER

MEAN SPRING AND NEAP CURVES

Springs occur 2 days after New and Full Moon.

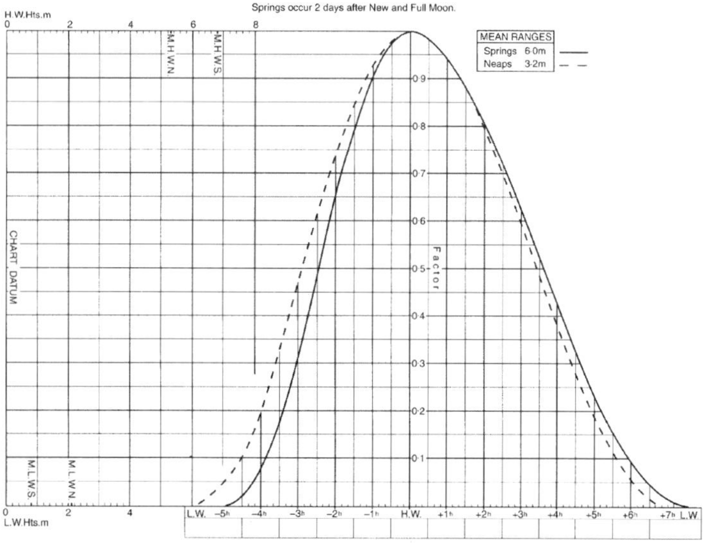

TILBURY

MEAN SPRING AND NEAP CURVES

Springs occur 3 days after New and Full Moon.

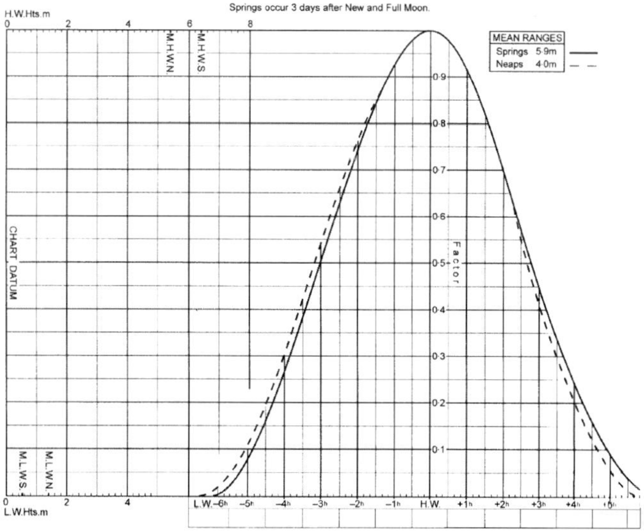

Appendix III

NAVIGATIONAL AIDS

GPS & DGPS

The GPS [Global Positioning System] is an aid to, but not a means of, navigation.

It is always incumbent on the navigator to check the suitability of the passage between one waypoint and another; it is also incumbent on the navigator to be aware of the possible cross-track errors! It is insufficient simply to enter the co-ordinates into the GPS, and then to rely on autohelm.

Mariners are advised that the operation and characteristics of GPS availability are under the control of the US Department of Defence. Signal availability and accuracy may be changed without warning.

As with all electronic navigation aids, signal reliability may be affected by extreme weather conditions and by interference [including jamming and spoofing]. The Author, on one disconcerting occasion in the Thames Estuary, encountered a temporary reversal of polarity!

The DGPS [Digital Global Positioning System] is derived from shore-based stations with a range of up to 50 nM around the coasts of the UK and the Republic of Ireland, with a 95% probability of accuracy to within 5 metres. The primary purpose is to monitor and correct the GPS; the enhanced accuracy is a secondary consideration.

The use of DGPS requires a suitable receiver; that receiver should also indicate if the DGPS service is unavailable. DGPS receivers are incompatible with other SBAS [Satelite Based Augmentation Systems].

[The notes on DGPS are extracted from the Trinity House 'Notice to Mariners No 2/13']

AIS

The intention of AIS [Automatic Identification Systems] is automatically to provide continuous information to other ships and to coastal authorities. The information provided relates to the identity of the ship, and its position, course, and speed over ground; other safety-related information may be included, but its display is dependent on the on-board equipment.

The SOLAS regulations require AIS to be fitted aboard 'all ships of 300 gross tonnage and upwards engaged on international voyages and all passenger ships irrespective of size'. [Regulation 19 of SOLAS Chapter V]. The Regulations were fully implemented in 2004, but there are limited exceptions.

There are advantages to small craft in the vicinity of shipping lanes, in that the identification of large vessels enables direct communication. This may be particularly valuable when the small craft is in the 'stand-on' position.

There is further comment in Appendix IV of this book, under 'Maritime Information', but the reception of AIS signals may be enabled by an inexpensive receiver linked to an on-board laptop.

Navtex

Navtex is a maritime information service, broadcast in textual format from land stations around the European coasts; the facility is dependent on a dedicated on-board receiver and antenna. The receiver, at entry level, is inexpensive and comprises a monochrome LED [or similar] screen of around 20cm width and which will accommodate around ten lines of message; larger screens with printout facility are available.

The UK broadcasts [NAVAREA I] are on the two frequencies of 490kHz and 518kHz. The receiver will not accept both at the same time, and it is necessary to toggle between the two according to the anticipated message times; it is possible to have two receivers, each dedicated to one frequency. The receiver may be set to accept [or disable] selected stations and types of message; in terms of UK southeastern waters, the relevant stations are Cullercoats [identifier 'U'], Niton [identifiers 'I' and 'K'], Oostende [identifer 'V'] and Corsen [France] [identifier 'A']; the messages relating to navigational, meteorological and piracy warnings [identifiers 'A', 'B' and 'D'] cannot be deselected, ice reports [identifier 'C'] usually should be deselected, weather forecasts [identifier 'E'] should be retained, as should real-time weather reports [identifier 'V']. In order to avoid interference among stations, the broadcasts are on staggered four-hourly timetables.

The UK 490kHz stations cover the area to about 12nM offshore, for the English and Irish coasts, and the European coast from Brest up to Oostende; Niton ['I'] and Cullercoats have some overlap. The messages contain detailed meteorological forecasts and related information.

Station	Broadcast Times [UT]					
Cullercoats ['U']	0320	0720	1120	1520	1920	2320
Niton ['I']	0120	0520	0920	1320	1720	2120

The 518kHz broadcasts serve a wider area. The Niton station [identifier 'K'] does not provide weather forecasts, and Oostende [identifier 'V'] provides forecasts and strong wind warnings for The Thames and Dover. Corsen [NAVAREA II] has some coverage of the English south coast.

Station	Broadcast Times [UT]					
Niton ['K']	0140	0540	0940	1340	1740	2140
Corsen ['A']	0000	0400	0800	1200	1600	2000
Oostende ['V']	0200	0600	1000	1400	1800	2200

The above notes are intended only as the most basic introduction to the facility.

Appendix IV

SOME INFORMATION SOURCES

Weather Forecasts

www.metoffice.gov.uk/weather
[National weather]
www.ioscc.org.uk
[Isle of Sheppey Sailing Club – useful links, and real-time local weather]
www.medwaycruisingclub.org.uk/weather.html
[real-time local weather]

Tidal Predictions

www.ntslf.org/tides
www.mobiletide.co.uk An inexpensive 'app' for smartphones

Notices to Mariners

Hydrographic Office	www.ukho.gov.uk/nmwebsearch/
Trinity House	www.trinityhouse.co.uk/mariner_info
PLA	www.pla.co.uk/safety/regulations....
Medway Ports	peelports.co.uk/port-authorities/medway

Maritime Information

CNIS [Coastal Vessel Information Service] VHF Ch11
Broadcast every 60mins [30mins if visibility drops below 2nM] to give warnings of navigational difficulties [aimed primarily at the TSZ]
SI [Marine Safety Information] VHF Ch23, 84, 86

AIS The publication of freely available web-based real-time AIS information is strongly discouraged by the IMO, as being potentially detrimental to the safety and security of ships and port facilities.

Travel

National Rail	www.nationalrail.co.uk
	www.thetrainline.com
National Express	www.nationalexpress.com
Stagecoach	www.stagecoachbus.com
Kent Travel Line	www.kent.gov.uk/roads_and_transport
Public Transport Journey Planner	www.transportdirect.info

Tourism

Rye Tourism	www.visit1066country.com
	www.ryesussex.co.uk
Kent Tourism	www.visitkent.co.uk
	www.medway-maritimekent.co.uk

Notes

Appendix V

THE AUTHOR

Robert Crane was born in London in 1938. He was educated at the then Finchley Catholic Grammar school, failed miserably at Medical School, and then gained a degree in Estate Management; he was later elected to Fellowship of the Royal Institution of Chartered Surveyors.

He obtained a wide range of experience in London, before moving down to Chichester where he commenced his own practice. He had taken the view that estate agency and professional work were an uneasy combination, and his practice was accordingly of a purely professional nature; much of his work was related to building surveying and the managing of insurance claims. It was not long before he opened a second office, and for a while his was the only multi-branch practice of that nature in the region.

He first retired in 1988 and returned to London, where he was awarded a research degree whilst continuing with consultancy work. Whilst hitherto his sailing had been of an 'as and when' nature, he was now able to spend more time on the water, and developed his interest in pilotage and exploration.

He was married in 1968; he and his wife have two sons. His main interests, other than sailing, are parish work, Rotary and gardening.

THE AUTHOR PHOTO: PETER SERNA